Letters of a Russian Dissident:
Ivan Pouschine's Siberian Exile Correspondence

Anna Pouschine

Letters of a Russian Dissident:
Ivan Pouschine's
Siberian Exile Correspondence

Anna Pouschine

Academica Press
Washington – London

Library of Congress Cataloging-in-Publication Data

Names: Pouschine, Anna, 1996- author.
Title: Letters of a Russian dissident : Ivan Pouschine's Siberian exile correspondence / Anna Pouschine.
Other titles: Ivan Pouschine's Siberian exile correspondence
Description: Washington : Academica Press, [2019]. | Excerpts from letters are in Russian and in English translation. | Includes bibliographical references and index. | Summary: "The Russian nobleman Ivan Ivanovich Pouschine is most recognized for two achievements: his leadership role in the 1825 Decembrist uprising against Russia's tsarist government and his set of poignant memoirs about his dear friend Alexander Pushkin. Pouschine's historical and cultural significance, although often subtle, extends much further, however. After graduating from Tsar Alexander I's new Lyceum in 1817, Pouschine spent several years in the military and government service, serving as an officer and judge. All the while, he was an active leader of various secret societies in both St. Petersburg and Moscow that discussed the viability of a democratic government for Russia. He went on to become a key organizer of the resulting 1825 Decembrist uprising, for which he was sentenced to thirty years of harsh exile in Siberia. In exile, Pouschine involved himself in a variety of self-motivated pursuits: leading efforts to improve intellectual discourse in remote Siberia; managing the Decembrists' cooperative, and serving as the center of the exiles' social circle. In this book, Princeton scholar Anna Pouschine will explore her ancestor's correspondence by examining how his letters created personal fulfillment in a desolate environment at a difficult moment in his country's storied past"-- Provided by publisher.
Identifiers: LCCN 2019027426 | ISBN 9781680531817 (hardcover) | ISBN 9781680531961 (paperback)
Subjects: LCSH: Pushchin, Ivan Ivanovich, 1798-1859--Exile. | Pushchin, Ivan Ivanovich, 1798-1859--Correspondence. | Russia--History-- December Uprising, 1825. | Decembrists--Russia (Federation)--Siberia--Biography. | Exiles--Russia (Federation)--Siberia--Correspondence. | Siberia (Russia)--Biography.
Classification: LCC DK212.P87 P68 2019 | DDC 947/.073092--dc23
LC record available at https://lccn.loc.gov/2019027426

Copyright 2019 Anna Pouschine

Contents

Author's Note vii
Introduction 1
Chapter I: Decembrists 13
Chapter II: Lyceum Classmates 41
Chapter III: Family 63
Conclusion 87
Afterward 91
Works Cited 95
Notes 97

Author's Note

Ivan Ivanovich Pouschine captured my interest thanks to our family relationship: he was my great-great-great-great grandfather. Indeed, some of my fondest childhood memories involve sitting at the dining room table, eating blini on a cold winter night, and hearing older family members debate details of anecdotes from Pouschine's life – his Lyceum days with his dear friend Alexander Pushkin, his leadership role in the secret Decembrist societies, and his undaunted attitude toward exile. Just as the era in which he came of age – the period after Russia's victory over Napoleon – was a Golden Age for Russia, Pouschine himself serves as a source of great pride for our family. His righteousness and humility continue to leave a particularly strong impression on his descendants.

In writing this book, I sought to produce a selective biographical account that presented him with the intimacy of a family member. I am deeply grateful to my thesis advisor at Princeton, Professor Ilya Vinitsky, for recommending the framework of "emotional communities" to comprehend important facets of Pouschine's persona. This book is meant to offer an overview of his character in a dynamic and affectionate manner.

И.И. Пущину

Мой первый друг, мой друг бесценный!
И я судьбу благословил,
Когда мой двор уединенный,
Печальным снегом занесенный,
Твой колокольчик огласил.

Молю святое провиденье:
Да голос мой душе твоей
Дарует то же утешенье,
Да озарит он заточенье
Лучом лицейских ясных дней!

1825–1826

To I.I. Puschin

My first friend, my invaluable friend!
Even I blessed fate,
When the sounds of your carriage
Rang out in my solitary courtyard
Covered in sad snow.

I pray to holy providence:
May my voice give to your soul
That same consolation,
May it illuminate your confinement
With the light of the clear days of the Lyceum!

Alexander Pushkin
(Translation by Michael Wachtel)

Introduction

Ivan Ivanovich Pouschine is best known for two reasons: his leadership role in the 1825 Decembrist uprising and his poignant memoirs about his dear friend, Russia's national poet Alexander Pushkin. Pouschine's historical and cultural significance, although often subtle, extended far beyond these two biographical details. After graduating in 1817 from the Tsarskoe Selo Lyceum, a progressive school for noble boys founded by Tsar Alexander I, Pouschine spent several years in military and government service, serving as a lieutenant in St. Petersburg then as a judge in a minor Moscow court.

In his youth, Pouschine was an active leader of various secret societies in both St. Petersburg and Moscow, which discussed ideas for a more democratic government for Russia. He went on to become a key organizer of the 1825 Decembrist uprising, for which he was sentenced to thirty years of exile in Siberia. He served time in labor camps in Chita and Petrovsky, and then lived in seclusion in Yalutorovsk. In exile, Pouschine got involved in a variety of self-motivated pursuits: leading efforts to improve intellectual discourse in remote Siberia; managing the Decembrists' artel, a shared collection of charitable funds and scholarly documents; and serving as a pillar of the Decembrist social circle by corresponding with a wide variety of people. This book will focus on the last initiative – correspondence – and examine how it gave Pouschine personal fulfillment in a desolate environment.

Pouschine's correspondence, especially by the end of his Siberian exile in the 1850s, provides noteworthy insight into his own character as well as into the evolving worldview of his associates. This book will not discuss the nuances of Pouschine's political views, but will rather focus on his emotional state as expressed in and through his correspondence.

Unavoidably, Pouschine's outlook was shaped by his decades of exile. Over his thirty-one years in Siberia (1826-1857), he had two children, adopted new hobbies including gardening and translation, developed personal concern for his Siberian neighbors, and began courting his future wife, N. D. Fonvizina. These changes in Pouschine's personal circumstances revealed how friendship, even by correspondence, could overcome geographic and temporal distance to console him. It also provided emotional support to allow him to pursue noble and socially worthwhile projects.

Later in his exile, Pouschine struggled with loneliness and heavily relied on his correspondence for emotional comfort. Pouschine's time in settlements in Western Siberia resulted in distressing solitude: in 1849, for example, Pouschine appealed to Prince P. D. Gorchakov for permission for a trip to Turinsk. While this trip was officially for medical purposes, it was in fact more for Pouschine to visit friends.[1] Three distinct social groups provided Pouschine with consolation throughout his exile: fellow Decembrist exiles, Lyceum classmates, and family members. The means by which Pouschine achieved solace through these interactions differed remarkably from group to group, however.

To characterize Pouschine's affiliate groups, this thesis will rely on Emily Wang's descriptions of the Decembrist and Lyceum groups as emotional communities, as described in her dissertation, "Civic Feeling:

Pushkin and the Decembrist Emotional Community." I will introduce my own characterization for Pouschine's family, but Wang argues that the Decembrists formed an "emotional community," which accounted for the group's lasting unity. She defines an emotional community as "a group of people defined by a shared worldview and language founded on emotion – a subculture defined from an emotional perspective."[2] Wang argues that the Decembrists were a group unified by a common emotional vision for Russia than by a single political ideology. Wang's definition depends on Barbara Rosenwein's original definition of an emotional community, as "flexible, complex relations that might develop between various groups in a given place and time."[3]

This book challenges the "place and time" constraint, by demonstrating that Pouschine remained emotionally attached to these groups throughout his exile. He can be understood as a Decembrist given his ongoing commitment to improving Russia in a way that coheres with the views of the rest of the group well beyond his participation in the December 1825 uprising. This book will focus on correspondence with one member of each of the three groups: Decembrists, Lyceum classmates, and family. This framework enables us to view Pouschine's role in these emotional communities as lifelong commitments that he devotedly keep in good repair throughout his exile. We can thus consider Pouschine as an active participant in all three groups, despite his distance from many of their members.

Through their correspondence, the Decembrists offered emotional support by inspiring one another to champion their ideals through beneficial institutional reform. Wang characterizes the Decembrists as a group united by their shared "conviction that noble feelings were necessary for social improvement."[4] She defines their "emotional program" as follows: "by being the best men they could be, they would eventually help Russia."[5] The Decembrist revolt and its fallout indeed affected the life trajectories of these rebels, naturally resulting in a changed view of "social improvement."

After their failed revolution, the Decembrists remained committed to unifying values, but adapted their courses of action to the limited resources available to them in Siberia. They shifted away from advocating Russian society's progress through wide-reaching reform and high-level institutional change. Instead they focused their attention on improving their local Siberian communities directly. For example, the Decembrist I. D. Yakushkin built a school to educate Siberian children.[6] Accordingly, the emotional community's underlying values persisted as the Decembrists continued to pursue their shared aspirations to carry out beneficial civic reform.

In addition to remaining in contact with the Decembrist community, Pouschine was also in regular contact with members of numerous other circles of the St. Petersburg elite: his fellow Lyceum graduates and his family. Wang affirms that it is both possible and likely for an individual to identify with more than one emotional community, just as a high school student may identify as both a "nerd" and a "artist."[7] Pouschine presented himself differently depending on the group with which he was corresponding. His letters have different tones resulting from changes in his emotional outlook, style of prose, and thematic content of the letters. Thus, the letters to Decembrists, Lyceum graduates, and family provide us with various perspectives on Pouschine as he related to the differing emotional outlooks of the three spheres.

Pouschine's correspondence with his fellow Lyceum graduates revealed his celebratory, jovial spirit. He reminisced with his former classmates to revive his youthful joy as a distraction from his exile's hardship and solitude. Many graduates of Pouschine's Lyceum class, most notably Pushkin, lived in St. Petersburg and continued to engage one another intellectually in their professional lives. This community's emotional outlook was more ambiguous than that of the Decembrists. Wang broadly characterizes this group as "prankish,"[8] "libertine," and "playful."[9] Further, especially in their correspondence, they are unified by their belief in friendship as a noble cause,[10] a characterization that came to be known as the "Lyceum Spirit."

This book will define the "Lyceum group" slightly differently than Wang. It will refer to all Lyceum graduates who maintained emotional connections to their Lyceum memories and friendships rather than a circle of St. Petersburg intellectuals that included non-Lyceum graduates. This Lyceum group was emotionally unified by its members' interest in harnessing the power of arts and culture to elevate general sensibilities throughout Russia. Many Lyceum graduates, like Pouschine, developed serious, professional demeanors. Nonetheless, they still had nostalgia for their shared Lyceum experiences and relished its spirit. For example, Pouschine's class festively reunited every October 19 to celebrate the school's anniversary.[11] Lyceum alumni remained personally committed to one another, as well as to the Lyceum's culture, well beyond graduation.

This book will argue that a third group, Pouschine's family, also functioned as a consoling emotional community during his exile. The family was unique among Pouschine's communities, as family relations are inherent rather than elected. Pouschine was born into his family, while he chose to join the Decembrists and the Lyceum group. Additionally, Pouschine's relations with his family were strained by his participation in the Decembrist revolt and by the birth of his illegitimate children. Despite these tense relations, some members of Pouschine's family continued to correspond with him, and the family's emotional function with regard to Pouschine was similar to that of the Decembrists and the Lyceum graduates: they offered the emotional support that inspired him to serve the community.

The family further distinguished itself by focusing on private affairs; Pouschine family members primarily discussed each other's individual, personal well-being, whereas the other groups focused on the status of the broader community, often in an abstract sense.

This book further diverges from Wang's study in its use of letters, rather than poetry, as the literature under analysis. The familiar letter's adaptability and forthright discourse provide a clear understanding of Pouschine's relationship to his emotional communities. The familiar letter is a highly versatile genre as it allows a wide variety of conversations. Pouschine's correspondence was far-reaching: he not only wrote many letters, but also wrote to individuals from varied backgrounds. This breadth of his correspondence gave Pouschine a wide perspective on the period's intellectual discourse. The genre also allows a pointed focus, as letters are personalized to the interests of the writer and recipient. This relatively private nature of communication also enabled varied and largely unrestricted discussion. Familiar letters were written to specific recipients, though authors keep their value to posterity in mind.[12] This book embraces letters as a vital empirical source by analyzing correspondence to gain biographical insight.[13] Pouschine's correspondence enabled him to play with his self-characterization and express himself differently in conversation with different groups.

Familiar letters served Pouschine's socializing intentions evident in the demonstration of friendship inherent in this type of correspondence. In his book *The Familiar Letter as a Literary Genre in the Age of Pushkin*, the eminent Russian Literature scholar William Mills Todd notes that friendship as a value in and of itself was a key reason for the popularity of letter writing among early nineteenth-century Russian intellectuals. He describes the familiar letter's amenability to translating friendship into literature: "[The familiar letter is] the genre most suited to the rejection of the official, panegyric literature on the one hand and immediate commercial success on the other. Friendship between author and reader spread to other genres as well."[14] Letters facilitated a shift in tone for the author and reader relationship from that of teacher and pupil to that of friends on equal footing. Accordingly, the genre of familiar letter became popular, for it valued the relationship between reader and writer over stylistic conventions.

Authors escaped the expectations of declaratory statements or the obligation of gratifying a broad audience. This tie between the familiar letter and the important role of friendship among Russian intellectuals is reflected in Pouschine's use of correspondence to find and explore purpose in his exile by seeking dialogue with others rather asserting his personal beliefs. Pouschine, however, develops this idea by exhibiting how letters can sustain three different kinds of friendships across his emotional communities.

Letters also suited the interests of emotional communities as a whole, thanks to their ability to bolster shared ideals. Todd attests to the familiar letter's ability to reaffirm common values effectively via its direct nature. He describes the Arzamasian's use of the familiar letter to affirm Enlightenment ideas – particularly "learning and civility" – from author to both reader and posterity:

> Civility and literacy . . . must be communicated to the reader by example, by the illustration of their pleasures and benefits, and by the involvement of the reader in them as a participant; hence the relationship of friendship between narrators and their created readers that we observed earlier. Familiar letters occupy a central position in such a process of enlightenment. The epistolarian generally appears cloaked in this harmonious ideal of learning and civility . . . but for the larger public he does so indirectly, in writing for his friend, not in an openly didactic, sermonical fashion.[15]

Todd frames familiar letters as an art form by outlining their ability to influence an audience through upholding key values. They impart artistic enlightenment in two ways. First, they effect the reader directly through personalized information that engages them as an active "participant" and "friend." Second, the semblance of friendship softens the message for the greater public, thus using the "cloak" of the "harmonious ideal of learning and civility" to attract a sympathetic attitude from an onlooker. The ability of the familiar letter to enlighten a wider audience makes it a perfect vehicle for furthering Pouschine's general cause, which was forwarding the progress of Russian culture. In addition to cementing friendships, he was able to celebrate the values of his communities in an intellectual manner. Throughout the analysis, this thesis will focus on the relationship between epistolarian and reader, rather than on the one between epistolarian and posterity.

Finally, the familiar letter suited Pouschine's personal desires given its ability to maintain interpersonal contact. At this time, Pouschine seemed keen to use correspondence to overcome solitude. Pouschine, unlike many of the St. Petersburg-based intellectuals who did not share his fate of exile, faced very limited social opportunities in his daily life. Accordingly, letters were a key basis for his social contact. Pouschine valued and took pristine care of the letters he wrote – keeping copies for himself, which he bound and often revisited. In contrast, the Arzamasians typically assumed that their recipients would preserve the letters and took much less bother.[16.] Pouschine's dedication to preserving and memorializing these communications indicated the high value he placed on individual friendships. His letters allowed him both to give and receive personal attention. Preserving his correspondence became an intellectual activity of its own as Pouschine amassed an ever larger and more valuable collection of discourse.

While earlier scholarship has tended to characterize emotional communities as a whole, this book will analyze the relationships between one individual and his affiliated communities. It will explore how belonging to such emotional communities benefited Pouschine by providing him consoling senses of personal purpose, especially late in his exile as his isolation wore on. Each of the groups will be discussed in its own chapter consisting of five sections: The "background" introductions will provide relevant information about how Pouschine's relationship to the group was shaped. The "emotion" sections will discuss the underlying feelings that Pouschine expresses in the letters, which often appear to gratify the emotional community. The "style" sections will explore how Pouschine conveys this emotion through his language and stylistic choices. The "content" sections will investigate events or activities that provide moments of fulfillment. Finally, the conclusion will summarize the emotional community's distinguishing features.

This book will also explore how Pouschine's emotional communities distinctly inspired him to engage Siberian society generally. In addition to displaying similar emotional outlooks, all three groups displayed an interest in improving life in Siberia, at least at the local level. Yet the means by which they carried out this objective differed. The exiled Decembrists largely focused on evaluating political reforms to improve the region's institutions. The Lyceum group utilized art to advance Siberian culture and elevate the region's general cultural consciousness. Finally, Pouschine's family protectively addressed the soulful well-being of dear friends and relatives to garner active sympathy throughout the community. Pouschine relied on these groups for emotional understanding; they ultimately provided fulfillment through their ability to inspire personal purpose in him.

Pouschine himself celebrated the sense of purpose he attained from this correspondence. He affirms his view of letter writing as a source of pleasure. He wrote in the spring of 1845 to the former director of the Lyceum, Engelhardt:

> «Сношения с родным, друзьями утешительны. Надобно быть в Сибири, чтобы настоящим образом понять эту отраду. В эти годы накопилась целая библиотека добрых листков–погодно переплетены. Считайте сами, сколько томов составилось. Часто заглядываю на эту полку с усладительным чувством. Судьба меня балует дружбою, мною не заслуженной. Сколько около меня товарищей, которые лишены даже родственных сношений: снятые эполеты все уничтожили, как будто связи родства и дружбы зависят от чинов и прочих пелендряхов»![17]
>
> Relations with family and friends are comforting. It is necessary to be in Siberia, in order to genuinely

understand this pleasure. In these years, a whole library of friendly leaflets has accumulated-they are bound annually. Consider yourself how many volumes have been composed.

Often I glance at this shelf with a feeling of delight. Fate pampers me with friendship, which I do not deserve. How many people around me who are deprived of even kindred relations: the removed epaulets destroyed all, as if family and friendly connections depend on rank and other shrouds!

Correspondence thus affected Pouschine meaningfully by providing him the gratifying sensation of friendship. He described his supreme value of these relationships by describing himself as being "pamper[ed]" by "fate." He presented his friendships as divine gifts associated with the spiritual realm. As a result, he proved this magnanimous attitude by relying on these relationships to carry out beneficial action. Through correspondence, Pouschine primarily connected with his friends over their shared support for noble causes, or endeavors that advanced the community's common values. Correspondence thus enabled Pouschine to maintain a sense of purpose in his exile, as the emotional consolation of friendship emboldened him to serve a righteous role in his Siberian community.

Chapter I: Decembrists

The Cross of Shackles

Background

The Decembrist Revolt of 1825 played a significant role in Russian history, as it was an early attempt to bring progress to the Russian political system by implementing enlightened ideals. Many of the leaders of the uprising were among the first Russians to receive classical Western educations, and many had been army officers who personally experienced European life and sensibilities during or after the Napoleonic Wars. Their exposure to post-revolutionary European intellectual discourse captured their interest as students, intellectuals, and potential leaders. The patriotic spirit aroused by Russia's victory over Napoleon glorified a sense of duty to country among the young elites.[18]

The Decembrist revolt combined these dual interests in intellectual advancement and patriotic duty. Devotion to heroic causes became prominent among the Russian intelligentsia in the late eighteenth century thanks to the Freemasons, who believed that noble sentiments bred noble individuals, who would actively pursue social improvement for the benefit of all.[19] The Decembrists expanded these ideas by including militaristic action in their endeavors, in the hope of implementing influential and lasting change.[20] Their aspirations culminated in a revolt that took place shortly after the death of Tsar Alexander I. Occurring in December 1825, it opposed Alexander's conservative younger brother Nicholas I and used a succession crisis as a pretext to implement a constitutional government by force. The revolt was disorganized and quickly suppressed, however. Five Decembrist leaders were hanged, and about two hundred others were banished to Siberia, often for life. But even in their exile, the Decembrists remained active citizens and proved committed to improving Russian society.

Viewing the Decembrists as an "emotional community" allows for analysis of Pouschine both as a Decembrist and as a distinct individual within the Decembrist community. Wang characterizes the Decembrist emotional community in reference to its devotion to improving Russia through a variety of means – political, educational, and intellectual. While the revolt primarily reflected their political ambitions, the Decembrists' objectives for progress spanned a variety of subjects. Wang encapsulates the breadth of their goals by defining their "emotional program" as a broad and gallant worldview: "by being the best men they could be, they would eventually help Russia."[21] The Decembrist mindset was centered on using active, courageous service to encourage beneficial reform. Pouschine's own position was notable as he expressed significant concern for the personal, as opposed to solely the intellectual, well-being of other Decembrists: he saw friendship as inherently valuable, not merely an instrument of change. Further, his actions were marked by remarkable disruption as he regularly defied expectations while implementing his ideas.

A key tenet of Decembrists belief held that the purpose of friendship was to enable such civic change. The Decembrists valued "noble" friendship relationships that promoted civic purposes over romantic love and flirtation.[22] They aspired to friendships that would result in "mutual self-improvement and virtue," emboldening them to become better selves and citizens.[23] Pouschine's correspondence in the 1850s provides insight into how this view evolved by the end of the Decembrists' lives. While their revolutionary drive had evolved since the uprising, they still remained highly concerned with Russia's political and social progress. Their discussion of the development of Russian life is notable for the personal attitudes towards Russia's progress; the correspondence reveals that the Decembrists still formed connections through their shared support of progressive institutions, while jointly distancing themselves from entities of which they disapproved.

Pouschine began developing his political beliefs while a student at the Tsar's Lyceum. His teachers attested to his intellectual curiosity; they described him as a diligent student who graduated "worthy of a silver medal."[24] In 1814, he embarked on his active dedication to his ideas by attending secret society meetings along with Lyceum classmates A. A. Delvig, Prince S. G. Volkonsky, and W. K. Kiukhelbeker.[25] The students joined the «Священной Артели» ("Sacred Artel"), a pre-Decembrist secret society that discussed many revolutionary themes. Pouschine explained that the potential for beneficial change intrigued him:

> «Постоянные наши беседы о предметах общественных, о зле существующего у нас порядка вещей и о возможности изменения, желаемого многими втайне, необыкновенно сблизили меня с этим мыслящим кружком».[26]
>
> Our continuous discussion about public subjects, about the evil that exists in our order of things, and about the possibility of change, desired by many in secret, thoroughly drew me into this intellectual circle.

The society thus served to spark the boy's interest in questioning the prevailing order and discussing defiant themes. At this young age, he began developing a critical view of the Russian government and integrating his ideas into subversive discussion.

After the students' 1817 Lyceum graduation, the society evolved into the «Союз Спасения» ("Union of Salvation"), which took action to realize their ideals. The society used the concept of communal artels, popular among officers at the time, to "improve one's material position."[27] Upon entering this organization, Pouschine expressed his hope that such an endeavor could have a widespread effect on Russian society:

> «Убежденный в горестном положении отечества моего, я вступил в общество в надежде, что в совокупности с другими могу быть России полезен слабыми моими способностями и иметь влияние на перемену правительства оной».[28]
>
> Assured of the sorrowful state of my country, I entered the society in hope that, together with others, I may benefit Russia with my weak abilities and have influence on change for its government.

Pouschine displays his adherence to Decembrist noble purpose through this affirmed dedication to reforming Russia. This idealistic, hopeful attitude contrasts with his misgivings towards the government later in his exile.

Nonetheless, his dedication to benefitting Russia actively enabled Pouschine to enter into the Decembrists' emotional community.

As a young man, Pouschine also served his country lawfully by serving in the prestigious Horse Guard of the Imperial army; however, he showed tension with the established authority. It seems that Pouschine may have left his post because of a dispute with his commander that arose from an insignificant omission of Pouschine on a form.²⁹ This experience exhibits Pouschine's preference to effect Russia with disruptive change, rather than traditional service.

After resigning from the post, he dedicated himself to the secret «Союз Благоденствия» ("Society of Prosperity"), which called for the members to commit themselves to practical doings in one of four industries: philanthropy, education, justice, or social economy.³⁰ Pouschine surprised both his acquaintances and other members of the society by choosing to take a post as a judge in the disreputable Moscow outdoor court–a shocking decision for such an educated, elite man.³¹

Pouschine's scandalous decision had numerous motivating factors that reflected his deep loyalties to the Decembrist objective of implementing enlightened ideas. Officially, as he explained during his interrogations after the uprising, Pouschine claimed that he sought court work to make a meaningful difference in Russian society:

> «Находясь в здешней Палате сверхштатным членом без жалованья и получа уже некоторый навык в производстве дела, я вознамерился найти место, где бы я мог с некоторым пособием со стороны правительства быть употреблен с пользою».³²
>
> Being in the local chamber as an extraneous member without a salary and already attaining several experiences in performing this job, I decided to find a place, where I, with some assistance from the government, would be employed beneficially.

This explanation–that the poorly managed and disreputable low courts offered an advantageous opportunity for beneficial change – exhibits Pouschine's wholehearted dedication to implementing the patriotic Decembrist ideal of serving the Russian people. In addition to his official reason for choosing the post – public service – he had a covert reason, which was to recruit Muscovite intellectuals to the revolutionary cause thereby reviving the southern branch of the "Northern Society."[33] Pouschine thus established his twofold function in the Decembrist initiative: carrying out direct action and fostering supportive personal relations.

Throughout his life, Pouschine's correspondence continued to explore this theme of using emotional connections to support action for common interests.

Within the Decembrists, he distinguished himself as someone who had strong ability to arouse the active support of others. Leading up to the revolt in 1825, Pouschine exhibited his strong managerial abilities by rapidly mobilizing the revolutionary group to action. He amassed the input of key supporters in Moscow and St. Petersburg to develop a written constitution for a new government.[34] Further, he eagerly advocated carrying out the revolution during the discontinuity in government after Alexander I's death, rapidly inciting revolutionary fervor among the groups.[35] Before the uprising, Pouschine carried himself with calm confidence: he did not consider the possibility of defeat and inspired a similar optimism in other leaders.[36] He planned to enter into the square with two other leading conspirators, Trubetskoy and Ryleev, to demand that the Senate accept their manifesto, which called for the abolition of autocracy, establishment of an interim government, the release of peasants from serfdom, and the introduction of freedom of speech.[37] On December 14, 1825, he honored his intentions resolutely, directing soldiers until the very end of the failed uprising. Fellow Decembrist A. E. Rosen described his lasting dedication:

«Всех бодрее в каре стоял И. И. Пущин, хотя он, как

отставной, был не в военной одежде, но солдаты охотно слушали его команду, видя его спокойствие и бодрость».[38]

I. I. Pouschine stood in the square more vivaciously than all others, although he, as a retired officer, was not in military clothing, soldiers readily listened to his commands, seeing his composure and vivacity.

Pouschine thus distinguished himself as a leader who acted on his intentions, both privately within the secret societies and publicly, in opposition to the established political regime.

In addition to his devotion to his political ideals, Pouschine retained a loyal attitude towards his fellow Decembrists, as he protected them faithfully after the uprising. When a Lyceum friend offered a forged passport that would have allowed him to escape, Pouschine reportedly refused to abandon his cohort by fleeing the country. He treated his co-conspirators protectively by refraining from informing on them; he invented fictitious members of such societies to confuse the police investigation.[39] Moreover, he benefited the group emotionally by uplifting the failed revolutionaries' spirits.

His character was not weakened by the harsh circumstances of imprisonment in St. Petersburg's notorious Peter and Paul Fortress. In fact, according to Rosen's testimony, Pouschine even brightened the mood in trial:

«И. И. Пущин по обыкновению был весел и заставил громко хохотать целый собравшийся кружок».[40]

I. I. Pouschine by habit was cheerful and made the whole assembled circle laugh loudly.

This note reflects Pouschine's personal concern for the other revolutionaries. His support for the group's emotional standing exemplifies the revolutionaries' deep care for one another, substantiating the strong bonds that exist within this emotional community.

Once in exile, Pouschine received emotional consolation by sustaining such relationships, with Decembrists near and far. Over his thirty-year exile, Pouschine moved through various places in Eastern Siberia: Chita in 1828–1830, Petrovsky in 1830–1839, Turnik in 1839–1843, and finally Yalutorovsk in 1843–1856. He gained a reputation as not only a source of support for fellow Decembrists, but also as an individual willing to help local people.[41]

The Decembrist N. V. Basargin noted of Pouschine:

«Его прямодушие, честность, в высшей степени бескорыстие высоко ставили его в нравственном отношении».[42]

His straightforwardness, honesty, unselfishness in the highest degree placed him highly in moral sense.

Indeed, Pouschine occupied his time in Siberia by caring for fellow Decembrists. Pouschine even received the nickname «Маремьяна» ("Maremyana"), a folkloric reference to a proverb that describes a deeply sympathetic individual, who is "sad for all."[43] Pouschine demonstrated this compassion through various projects to improve the Siberian communities. While among other Decembrists in the Chita prison, he organized the "small artel" of charitable funds to aid poor Decembrists in their transition to Siberia.[44] When in exile in remote settlements, he circulated books and newspapers to care for his comrade's intellectual needs. Accordingly, Pouschine distinguished himself with his willingness to take direct action to support fellow Decembrists.

Ivan Dmitriyevich Yakushkin's correspondence with Pouschine illuminated Pouschine's devotion to noble duties. Before the uprising, Yakushkin served in the Russian Imperial Guards and participated in the military campaigns of 1812, 1813, and 1814. These endeavors piqued his interest in the progress of Russia, as he became exposed to his native land's shortcomings compared to those of the West.[45] As he wrote in his memoirs:

> «Вероятно в первый раз обратило внимание моё на состав общественный в России и заставило видеть в нём недостатки. По возвращении из-за границы крепостное состояние людей представилось мне как единственная преграда сближению всех сословий и вместе с сим общественному образованию в России».[46]

> Probably for the first time my attention was drawn to the public body in Russia and was compelled to see the weaknesses in it. On my return from abroad, the status of serf people seemed to me as the only barrier to the convergence of all classes, this together with public education in Russia.

Both Decembrists felt inspired to improve Russia after exposure to foreign systems; however, Yakushkin experienced European societies firsthand in active military campaigns, while Pouschine learned of ideas passively in the Lyceum. As a result, Yakushkin's military training (and lack of a formal education) distinguished him from members of the more artistic, lighthearted Lyceum circles. In the correspondence, Yakushkin appeared committed to enacting civic reforms to improve Siberian society. Yakushkin's perspective thus aptly adhered to the Decembrist cause.

Taken as a whole, Pouschine's correspondence with Yakushkin by the end of their exile revealed the evolution of Decembrist ideals. Rather than planning reforms, the two friends used the correspondence to reflect on the results of their attempts to democratize enlightened ideals. Yakushkin and Pouschine first met when they joined the Union of Salvation in 1817 and continued their friendship throughout the exile, as they were together in the Chita prison and the Yalutorovsk colony. According to family legend, their friendship is represented by a cross Pouschine welded for Yakushkin from broken shackle links. (The cross is currently on display in the State Historical Museum in Moscow.)

In his exile in Yalutorovsk, Yakushkin acted on his dream of democratized public education by establishing a men's school in 1842 and women's school in 1850.[47] Such active devotion to his personal beliefs illustrated Yakushkin's shared ethos with the Decembrist emotional community. The schools themselves proved incredibly popular and successful, educating a large number of children.[48] This unyielding dedication to noble action comprehensively demonstrated Yakushkin's faithful commitment to that Decembrist ideal. With his longstanding participation in secret societies, poignant friendship with Pouschine, and active devotion to noble causes during his exile, Yakushkin provided a good example of what it means to put Decembrist principles into action. Further, his serious tone throughout the letters well exemplified Wang's characterization of the Decembrist emotional community as "sincere."[49]

Decembrist Emotion: Triumph

The Decembrists regarded friendship as a means of support for carrying out noble action; accordingly, they provided emotional support to one another by honoring accomplishments and triumphs. In the letters, triumph emerges as a feeling of achievement from recognizing the successful results of worthy civic labors. The exiled Decembrists collectively aimed to advance governance throughout Russia; consequently, their correspondence is centered on the developments of such endeavors for the improvement of Siberian society. The two friends,

Pouschine and Yakushkin, displayed strong mutual understanding in their pursuit of advancement. Pouschine regularly expected Yakushkin to have a likeminded outlook. They engaged each other by discussing triumph in a variety of forms: their own achievements of triumph, the triumphant moments of others, and the apparent absence of triumph in Russian politics. Thus, Pouschine and Yakushkin provided each other with consolation through sympathetic celebrations of the successes of their labor.

Pouschine initially evidenced the Decembrists' collective triumph by confirming their ability to implement successful governance in Siberia. First, Pouschine proudly reported on their organized efforts to administer their Siberian settlement:

> «Третьего дня с кафедры прочел ваш листок от 26-го сентября. Это была суббота, следовательно, вся наша артель слушала меня и все мы порадовались, что благополучно совершилось ваше демократическое путешествие».[50]

> On the third day, from the pulpit, I read your leaflet from September 26. It was Saturday, therefore, our entire artel listened to me and we were all glad that your democratic journey was smoothly accomplished.

In this comment, Pouschine confirmed the united efforts of the Decembrists' artel, which served as their governing body in Siberia. He established his own stately role as he read "from the pulpit." He further noted the artel's active response the news: they "listened" and were "glad" of the report. They demonstrated their political inclinations as they specifically supported the "democratic journey." The group appeared pleased by the confirmation that the journey was "accomplished" and thus satisfied by the successful result. This description of the Decembrists' active governing efforts revealed that the group was unified by their pursuit of achievement.

Pouschine further celebrated the Decembrists' ability to have recognizable effect on the socioeconomic standing of Siberian civilians. Without referencing a specific Decembrist endeavor, he gladly reported on the observable improvement of the community in Yalutorovsk:

> «Станции необыкновенно улучшились. Поразило меня, что только одного нищего встретили по всей дороге досюда».[51]
>
> The stations have improved remarkably. It struck me that only one beggar was met all the way here.

Pouschine celebrated the notable advancement of the Siberian community. Though he did not directly attribute this "improve[ment]" to a Decembrist project, by sharing the observation with Yakushkin he implied its relevance and suggested that their group contributed to this result. Pouschine further displayed his constant attention to the social status of Siberian inhabitants, as he found the change "remarkable" and it "struck" him. Such keen observations revealed Pouschine's desire to notice the results of their triumphant actions. He appeared to attain pleasure through recognizing the beneficial outcomes of the Decembrists' efforts, and anticipated that the news would gladden Yakushkin as well.

The Decembrists also attained triumph through confirmation that they had emboldened others to continue to carry out beneficial, active service. Yakushkin appeared gratified by the assurance that his former students were actively devoted to social and political support. Pouschine informed him of the success of his former student Finochka's new husband:

> «Теперь поехал хлопотать, чтоб его перевели сюда начальником кавалерии. Все его хвалят, говорят, что человек скромный и трезвый. Поздравьте вашу

ученицу».⁵²

Now he went to petition, so that they transfer him here as chief of cavalry. Everyone praises him, saying, that he is a humble and sober man. Congratulate your student.

Pouschine applauded his success by calling Yakushkin to act: "congratulate your student." This praise for admirable actors established the Decembrists' commitment to righteous action. Pouschine further saluted the husband's political contribution, highlighting his professional success as "chief of cavalry" as well as his commendable "modest and sober" reputation. The Decembrists thus valued a man for both his effect on society, as well as his ability to live life in a moral way. Pouschine also sought praise for Finochka's social devotion. As a wife, she appeared to committed to her husband, and by extension, to his beneficial service to society. Pouschine expected that his report of Finochka's promising family life and her devotion to such a strong citizen would gratify Yakushkin, who was deeply committed to the education of native Siberian children. Between themselves, the Decembrists further encouraged such commitment to benefiting society through bestowing their own active praise.

In contrast to the celebration of Yakushkin's influence over others, Pouschine exhibited his own modesty by describing his children's development objectively and humbly. Pouschine honored his children's accomplishments, yet his tone lacked any expectation of praise for his family's pursuits:

«Ваня всякий день в училище женском. Толкует уже два десятка и ничего единиц. Аннушка с меня ростом. Задает концерты с Берхом a quatre mains».⁵³

Vanya is at the women's school every day. He already counts two dozen with no kind of units. Annushka is growing with me. She does piano duets with Berkh.

In reporting on his children, Pouschine remained detached. Rather than describing emotional relationships, he positioned his children as independent actors. He underscored their dedication to intellectual advancement, reflecting the Decembrist's value of embracing progressive ideals. On the one hand, Vanya received an education at the school, preparing him to be a solid citizen. Pouschine's account emphasized Vanya's effort -- the boy spends "every day" pursuing education, and can now count "two dozen" units. The awkward phrasing of «ничего единиц» ("of no units") likely acknowledged the son's errors as he begins to count.

This improper writing suggests that Pouschine was humbly relating himself to his son, expressing a lack of judgment in his son's struggles. Pouschine also presented Annushka's success in domestic affairs. He confirmed that she was "growing" and attaining musical abilities by "playing concerts." He again reported on the success of the youths in gaining auspicious skills. However, he displayed his own humility in these accounts by focusing on his children's efforts rather than on his own efforts as a parent. He did not mention his own involvement, but rather positioned his children for triumph on their own. Such a stoic description highlighted his children's capacity for intellectual advancement rather than their ability to provide personal, emotional comfort. Pouschine's portrayal of his children as hardworking suggests that Yakushkin could best relate to them through recognition of their accomplishments.

In addition to celebrating moments of achievement, the friends also discussed aspects of society that showcased a lack of triumph, marked by hindrances to Russia's advancement. In corresponding with

Decembrists, Pouschine revealed a pessimistic distrust of the Russian government. His expressions of triumph thus juxtaposed these apprehensive comments on Russia's future. Pouschine, however, described his doubt emotionally; perhaps fearing the censors, he refrained from articulating his criticism. For example, Pouschine wrote of his general discontent in response to various reports:

>«Вообще все это мрачно и мрачны последние телеграфические депеши о Корфе, флоте, подошедшем к Одессе, и высадке Омер-Паши в Азиатскую Турцию».[54]
>
>In general, all is somber and the last telegraphic dispatches about Korf, the fleet approaching Odessa, and the landing of Omer-Pasha in Asiatic Turkey are grim.

Pouschine revealed his dismay with Russia's military endeavors with sensational descriptions – "grim" and "somber." This tone revealed a certain pessimism, and distanced him from the events through such moody, almost poetic, expressions. This dissociation indicates a lack of inspiring triumph. At the time, the Russian government had a floundering reputation: the army faced military defeats, the war caused economic strain on the country, and the conflicts highlighted Russia's backwardness compared with the rest of Europe.[55] Yet despite his political knowledge and involvement, Pouschine indicated his dissatisfaction with Russia's position by expressing himself sentimentally. His commentary served as evidence of his emotional connection with Yakushkin: they used emotional discussion to attain mutual understanding even when discussing complex, political themes.

In addition to proving his connection to Yakushkin through doubts, he also established distance between himself and the Tsar to show continuing dissatisfaction with the political regime. Pouschine focused his criticism on the Tsar's personal decisions and lack of beneficial outcomes. As he commented on Tsar Alexander II's decision to release his final conversation with his father, Tsar Nicholas I, publicly:

> «За одно не спасибо ему, что он передал гласности последние слова отца, вспомнившего нас и при гробе. Кажется, сыну следовало бы оставить при себе такое чувство умирающего отца. Мне на его месте совестно бы было поставить весь мир свидетелем такой беседы».[56]

> For one, do not thank him for delivering the last words of his father, remembering us even on his deathbed, to the public. It seems the son ought to keep this feeling of the dying father to himself. In his place, I would feel self-conscious to make the entire world an onlooker to such a conversation.

Pouschine condemned the new ruler's emotional responses. He pointed to a poignant moment – a father and son's final conversation – to express disagreement with the government and its scenario of power. The scene was emotional, for it revealed the new Tsar's "feelings" in a way that Pouschine found unseemly. Pouschine distinguished himself from the Tsar with his own sense of "self-consciousness," suggesting that revealing such intimate details was tasteless or shameful. His disparaging attitude indicated the Tsar's discord with the Decembrists' emotional worldview, which was more stoic and prized the public interest over personal considerations. Given the Decembrists' adherence to friendship to encourage noble action in society, Pouschine here displayed a corruption of that view: that the Tsar's revelation of an intimate personal moment had been an embarrassment to himself and the nation and therefore outside the Decembrists' emotional community. Nonetheless, Pouschine's open discussion of emotion further confirmed his intimacy with Yakushkin.

Though the Decembrists' friendships originated in shared

revolutionary ideals, they used emotions to accentuate their stately discourse. They most strongly connected over felicitous indications of society's advancement. Pouschine's reports of good news ranged in tone from excited to stoic, and he consistently applauded achievements that resulted from the application of Decembrist ideals to Siberian society. It also reaffirmed the bonds of the Decembrist's emotional community. In addition to using a shared, emotional understanding to express abstract thoughts, they acknowledged their emotional critique of Russia's political regime. Overall, their correspondence regarding the results of their efforts honored their unrelenting dedication to the Decembrists' "noble" purposes.

Decembrist Style

In corresponding with the Decembrists on general matters, Pouschine's tone was primarily earnest, reflecting his and by extension, their, grand ambitions. However, he subtly revealed his care for certain entities by juxtaposing this formal tone with a playful attitude. Throughout the letters, Pouschine treated Yakushkin cordially and wrote about objective, factual information in clear language. The letters reveal a great sense of assurance: Pouschine avoided superfluous wording and refrained from sentimental flourishes. For example, he signed his name with only a simple "I. P." This reserved tone could at first appear to obscure the emotional connection between him and Yakushkin. However, the juxtaposition of the extreme impersonal style used to describe institutions he regarded as "backward" with the playful quips and details used to describe entities of which he was fond introduces intriguing elements of emotional complexity. While his resolute determination characterized him as a Decembrist, he celebrated the triumphant resolve of others through compassionate descriptions of certain subjects.

Pouschine established his formal attitude by asserting that certain monumental events demanded attention and inhibited personal discourse. For example, he noted that responding to the death of the Tsar trumped normal friendly correspondence:

> «Я не берусь передавать вам длинную речь, тем более, что теперь такое новое событие, которое поглощает все мелочи вседневной нашей жизни, которую вы живо можете себе представить».[57]
>
> I do not intend to give you a long speech, especially, that now such a new event, which absorbs all little things of our daily lives, that you can imagine vividly.

The moment hindered Pouschine's ability to connect with his friend. He presents the event commandingly when he says it "absorbs all the little things of our daily life," suggesting his own reduced agency. Pouschine was subdued by the event, juxtaposing the gratifying effect of triumphant moments. He also used emotionally neutral language to indicate his aversion for the deceased Tsar, referring to his death only as a "new event." Such an ambiguous description suggested that Pouschine was uninterested in discussing the death on any deeply emotional level, despite the fact that it was Nicholas I who had sent him and his fellow rebels into decades of exile.

In contrast, Pouschine showed that the satisfaction of helpful accomplishment inspired animating joy. Pouschine amicably commented on his success in aiding Yakushkin:

> «Щадя вас, я не тотчас вам откликнулся, теперь предстоит случай, я воспользуюсь камер-юнкерским проездом, чтоб благодарить вас. Поручение ваше я исполнил, вместо одной руки поцеловал обе вашим именем».[58]

Sparing you, I did not immediately answer you, now I have a chance, I will use the *kammeriunker*'s[59] passage, to thank you. I executed your commission, instead of one hand I kiss both your names.

Pouschine thus presented elation by greeting Yakushkin affectionately. He emphasized his "kissing" of his old friend, and confirmed his reassured "thanks" for the correspondence. His vivacity marked a triumphant moment for Pouschine, who was enlivened by his active occupations in far less than ideal circumstances. Firstly, he actively carried out Yakushkin's requests. He both responded to Yakushkin's original letter and "executed his commission," showing that correspondence itself can at least appear to capture satisfying exploits. Secondly, Pouschine indicated his own preoccupations – as he could not "immediately respond"– to indicate his own, independent pursuit of achievement. Ultimately, this amicable greeting reflected the connection between friendship and achievement.

In addition to using affable language to indicate triumphant sentiments, Pouschine adopted a playful tone to describe meaningful friendship. He revealed the high value he assigned to these connections, thus reaffirming the Decembrist belief that noble friendship would inspire noble actions. For example, he satirized excessively poetic and melodramatic correspondence:

«Теперь в Ялуторовске, как бывало говаривал Маржаков, кой-где в наших окнах светит огонек. Полагаю, что и Матвей Апостол, отпраздновавши день Екатерины, тоже пустился за нами вслед».[60]

Now in Yalutorovsk, as Marzhakov used to say, light shines in our windows here-and-there. I believe, that Matthew the Apostle, having celebrated the day of Catherine, also set off behind us.

In this remark, Pouschine employed lofty language to describe his mundane life. The image "in our window light shines" satirically dramatized the letter's introduction. Such an aggrandized cliché juxtaposed the letter's intimate nature with a grand spiritual realm. His reference to "Matthew the Apostle" playfully referred to the fellow exiled Decembrist and close friend Matvei Ivanovich Murav'ev-Apostol'. While the comment appears as a jest, it nonetheless evokes the martyred image of Decembrists within a Christian connotation. Pouschine's aggrandizing of the man indicated his underlying respect, while the jocular tone of this remark again exhibited the Decembrists' intimate bonds.

In contrast to his reverent description of his friend, Pouschine referred to Nicholas I ambiguously, refraining from using his name or title. Instead, Pouschine described the tsar using vague associations and imprecise ideas:

> «Разумеется, очень естественно человеку, рожденному на свет, умереть–как царю, так и подданному, но умереть в такую минуту тому, который затеял всю кутерьму–это не совсем обыкновенно. Одним словом, этим многое может разрешиться».[61]

> Clearly, it is very natural for any person who was born, to die – be it a tsar or any subject of the tsar – but for the one who undertook this whole mess to die at such a moment – it is not entirely usual. In a word, a lot can be resolved.

He referred to the tsar impersonally as the "king" or with the pronoun "one." He thus subverted the Tsar's personality by portraying him solely as a figurehead or even as an abstraction. Pouschine further distanced himself by describing the situation without expressing an opinion, stating generally that "it's not entirely ordinary" and "a lot can be resolved." This vague discussion distanced him from any relationship to the event. Such generic statements seemed to hinder conversation, given the lack of insightful, stimulating ideas around them.

Throughout his correspondence, Pouschine built tension between affection and formality to express a subtle attitude toward subjects. On the one hand, he used playful language to establish an affectionate tone in his letters – he demonstrated how discussion of triumphant moments provided him with joyful consolation. At the same time, however, he noted that consequential political events, while causing distress, also demanded serious attention. Yet Pouschine ultimately confirmed his value of the underlying, personal relations: he remained primarily committed to building friendships that encouraged noble action. He indicated his value of others through expressions both affectionate to and aggrandizing to underscore the gratifying role of noble friendships.

Decembrist Content

The Decembrists' sense of friendship was primarily concerned with public rather than private life, as the men were united by their desire to bring about progressive change in Russia. Pouschine centered his letters on the era's key political developments, from broad national discourse – the 1855 death of Tsar Nicholas I – to developments within his limited Siberian community. Pouschine's generally stoic tone underscored the Decembrists' revolutionary ambitions; they remained devoted to Russia's advancement despite their own adversity. Given their advancing ages and diminished capabilities for influence, Pouschine and Yakushkin had a reduced ability to pursue revolutionary change. Nonetheless, in his letters, Pouschine still appeared interested in means that provided him a sensation of power. While he displayed great individual agency throughout the planning of the Decembrist Uprising, he later strove to attain a sense of active purpose by considering others' challenges, ranging from the Tsar's monumental causes to the humble efforts of common citizens. Pouschine presented a humble regard for triumph in a variety of forms, as he discussed moments of importance in a variety of areas. Accordingly, he attained a vicarious sense of purpose by writing of the potential for triumph throughout all levels of society.

Pouschine initially found the sensation of supreme, public power through writing from the Tsar's perspective. Unable to take action himself, he imagined the Tsar's responsibilities in ensuring the well-being of Russia as a whole:

> «Одним словам, этим многое может разрешиться. Новому правителю легче действовать и поправлять ошибки не свои. С другой стороны, и наши враги, может быть, поймут, что не к чему елозить и мучиться».[62]

> In a word, a lot can be resolved. It is easier for the new ruler to act and amend mistakes not his own. On the other hand, even our enemies, perhaps, will understand that there is nothing worth fussing about or suffering for.

At the time of Alexander II's succession to the throne in 1855, Pouschine underscored the new Tsar's need to carry out action. He described Russia's present state with a disparaging tone. He underscored the past Tsar's "mistakes," suggesting Russia's weaknesses in facing its "enemies," against whom it was still fighting the Caucasian War. However, he suggested that the new leader bore the onus of shaping Russia by passively observing, "a lot can be resolved." His vague commentary on the country's future made for an unsettling and inconclusive end to the observation. Pouschine also undermined the Tsar's heroism by indicating that "enemies" also held influence over Russia's future. Such meditations illustrated that Pouschine had a continuing interest in attaining a triumphant future for Russia as a whole, even as the tsarist system against which he had rebelled plodded along.

Secondly, Pouschine used his correspondence to assume Yakushkin's private power by helping his friend maintain his Siberian house. Pouschine wrote of his active management of Yakushkin's domestic matters, describing his assistance in the upkeep of Yakushkin's former home:

> «Поручила Федосья Родионовна просить вашего позволения снять со стены ситец. В нем просто образовались траншеи клопов, и беспрестанное нападение этих домашних врагов не дает им покою. Хотя бы меня не уполномочили на этот счет, но я им сказал, что могут действовать, не ожидая вашего разрешения».[63]

> Fedosya Rodionovna has requested your permission to remove the chintz from the wall. In it, trenches of bedbugs were simply forming, and relentless assaults on these domestic enemies did not give them peace. Although no one authorized me on this account, I said to them, that they can act, without waiting for your permission.

Pouschine displayed agency in protecting the Yakushkin household. He acknowledged that he stood in for Yakushkin's authority: "I said to them, that they can act, without waiting for your permission." Thus, Pouschine positioned himself in Yakushkin's commanding role, exhibiting the strong understanding between the two men. His take-charge decision underscored the resolute connection between the two men, as Pouschine proved confident in his ability to act in the best interests of those in the household. Furthermore, he portrayed himself in a heroic role in opposition to the dramatized "domestic enemies." Pouschine thus appeared proud of his active protection of his friend's home; his commitment to careful oversight demonstrated how friends' intimacy becomes reflected in active service.

Finally, Pouschine attained a sense of activity by writing about social progress in Siberian society. Pouschine here displayed especially humble concerns, commenting on the activity of Siberian families:

> «В Ялуторовске главная новость – замужество Финочки. Она после Пасхи выходит за Яновского, командира казаков в Тюмени».[64]
>
> In Yalutorovsk the main news is the marriage of Finochka. After Easter she goes to Yanovsky, for the commander of Cossacks in Tyumen.

Pouschine described society's progression by confirming the advancement of family life. He praised the newlyweds for having recognizably acted beneficially in society. He confirmed the importance of the new marriage by referring to it as "the main news." Further, he portrayed the bridegroom's service to society, by specifying his role in the army, rather than describing his sentimental connection to his wife.

Pouschine thus framed emotional connection as a means of supporting society's public endeavors. By likening the emotional triumph of marriage though the professional triumph of active service, Pouschine praised this instance of personal connection as a means of supporting noble action in society. His description of a bright young couple suggested a promising future not only for them, but for Russian society as a whole. Thus, while Pouschine did not act himself, his recognition of others' actions demonstrated his continued interest in social progress – he chose to celebrate this couple for their capacity to strengthen Russian society through noble service.

Pouschine also displayed a sustained desire for agency by

discussing opportunities to improve society through his correspondence. First, he adopted the Tsar's perspective to discuss the work ahead of Russia in order to increase its power as a country. This commentary evidenced Pouschine's continuing interest in Russia's political advancement. Second, he demonstrated his pragmatic, active support for his friends by assuming Yakushkin's domestic responsibilities. He appears to have gained satisfaction from forming a connection with his friend by actively concerning himself with domestic affairs, revealing the powerful intimacy between the two friends. Finally, Pouschine noted Siberia's social progress, commenting on the local community's work for a better future. He praised a native Siberian couple for their emotional dedication to each other through marriage, as well as for their dedication to society as a whole through the husband's military service. The humble nature of this comment thus indicated that Pouschine was interested in modest displays of service in addition to effective national politics. Thus, the Decembrists appear to have sustained their emotional connection by recognizing a need for valued noble action.

Conclusion

The correspondence among the Decembrists is notable for its focus on noble political action. By the end of their exile, their view of active support differed significantly from their idealistic goals as young revolutionaries. Their outlook on noble action had become more direct. Rather than aspiring to sweeping reform, as older men they focused on serving their local communities in Siberia, a foreshadow of the "small deeds" liberal ethos that would sweep the ranks of the Russian intelligentsia later in the nineteenth century. Although their capabilities had diminished by this later point in their lives, they still occupied themselves by recognizing personal triumphs in a variety of forms: sending congratulatory messages, discussing international affairs, and even addressing domestic maintenance issues. Such pursuits provided the Decembrists with gratification because they were able to continue contributing to Russian society despite the incredible adversity of their circumstances.

In correspondence, Ivan Pouschine and his fellow Decembrists confirmed their dedication to noble action through underlying emotion, style, and content. They proved dedicated to honoring each another's pursuit of triumphant moments, as they commiserated over emotional hardships, celebrated noteworthy achievements, and even acknowledged the continuing shortcomings of the political regime they had tried to overthrow.

Stylistically, their letters reveal emotional connection through affectionate regard. Although they tend to have a stoic tone, Pouschine's moments of stylistic play evidence the compassionate bonds among the Decembrist community. Finally, the content of the letters underscored the Decembrists' magnanimous nature. In the letters, they appear sincerely dedicated to serving society as a whole. While their letters lack pronounced displays of affection, they nonetheless referenced a common interest in civic action to substantiate emotional connections.

Ultimately, the Decembrists' correspondence expanded on their original revolutionary aims through emphasis on desired civic reforms. Compared to their original political intentions, the Decembrists now, three decades after the uprising, continued to express deep concern for other's personal development. Among their former students, children, and each other, the Decembrists' correspondence was at its most intimate and precise when discussing meaningful connections with others. Pouschine focused on fostering uplifting sensations with his comrades, and left his descriptions of displeasing institutions and people vague.

Chapter II:
Lyceum Classmates

The Lyceum Piano

Lyceum Background

Tsar Alexander I founded the Tsarskoe Selo Lyceum in 1811 to promote Russia's modernization and Westernization. He believed that establishing a group of classically educated Russians of noble background was necessary for realizing progressive reform.[65] Accordingly, the school exposed its students to the latest European intellectual works to compensate for Russia's relative backwardness. The first head of the school was V. F. Malinovsky, a well-known democrat and outspoken opponent of serfdom. He was a proponent of the belief in the equality of all people and intended his students to be highly active in addressing Russia's political shortcomings.[66] Malinovsky's belief in an emboldened role for citizens instilled that active mindset among the students. Professors taught that the natural rights of people are equal. For example, one course at the school emphasized the need for greater agency for individual citizens; the professor preached:

> «Люди, вступая в общество, желают свободы и благосостояния, а не рабства и нищеты».[67]

> People, stepping into society, want freedom and well-being, not slavery and poverty.

These ideas, supplemented by the latest works of Western

economics, philosophy, and politics, made powerful impressions on the students.

The striking disparity between Europe and Russia in terms of socio-political advancement rapidly became clear to them. The importance of their lessons highlighted the numerous historic events of the time, such as the War of 1812 and recent liberation of serfs in much of Europe.[68] All these influences combined to form an intensely patriotic spirit, which drove the students to be eager for parallel changes in Russia.

The school's primary aim was to inspire a patriotic devotion to advancing Russian society. Yet the Lyceum also sparked cherished friendships that engendered deep concern for one another. The school reportedly had a jovial atmosphere that enabled great intimacy among the students. As graduates, the men shared a high regard for their joyous Lyceum memories and accordingly treated each other with devout loyalty. Though the students embarked on a wide range of careers, they remained unified by a common desire for progress in Russian society through cultural advancement. These affectionate friendships proved to be highly meaningful for Pouschine, as they continued to console him throughout his exile. The Lyceum emotional community was distinct in its aims to propagate graduates' lifelong appreciation of intellectual life as developed from their school days.

While a student, Pouschine was a natural fit in the Lyceum and enjoyed strong academic and social success. Teachers applauded him for his thoughtfulness and diligence. He performed well across a variety of courses, including history, politics, and morality. As the Lyceum educator M. C. Piletsky observed of Pouschine's assiduous character:

«Благородство, воспитанность, добродушие,

скромность, чувствительность с мужеством и тонким честолюбием, особенно же рассудительность – суть отличные его свойства».[69]

Nobility, politeness, good nature, humility, sympathy, with courage and subtle ambition, particularly discretion – in essence these are his excellent qualities.

Pouschine's diligence was widely praised: when he graduated in 1817, he was deemed "worthy of a silver medal."[70] He was also well-liked by other students, with whom he enjoyed lifelong friendships. Most notably, he became dear friends with the future national poet Alexander Pushkin, with whom he often chatted through the windows of their side-by-side lodgings. The sincerity of the friendship was confirmed in 1825, when Pouschine visited his old friend, who was condemned to exile at his Mikhailovskoe estate near Pskov, and the old friends had a cherished, celebratory reunion. Their friendship was immortalized in various Pushkin poems and in Pouschine's *Notes on Pushkin*. Pouschine also created collegial relationships with future Decembrists Delvig, Volkhovsky, and Kiukhelbeker, with whom he began participation in early, pre-Decembrist secret societies. All of these relationships shared a common dedication to supporting intellectual advancement.

Throughout his time at the Lyceum, Pouschine spent much time at leisure and joking with fellow classmates. The Lyceum atmosphere, its "spirit," was marked by camaraderie. Even as professionals in St. Petersburg, members of the group replicated this spirit by occupying their time with indulgent amusements, engaging each other with lewd banter at elaborate parties.[71] Pouschine's class partook in an annual tradition of reuniting every October 19, the anniversary of their first day of school, which they celebrated as a holiday.[72]

The lighthearted tone of their reunions belied the Lyceum graduates' loyal attitude towards friendship. Pouschine's correspondence showed the power of these friendships, as the group fondly transmitted joy through bonding over their shared concern for Russian culture.

Pouschine's personal outlook, rooted in amicability and pride in his country, positioned him centrally within the Lyceum's intellectual elite. Even his cantankerous classmate and later sharp critic of the Decembrists, Baron M. A. Korf, had fond memories of Pouschine's acceptance in the Lyceum class:

> «Один из тех, которые наиболее любимы были товарищами, с светлым умом, с чистою душой, он имел почти те же качества, как и Есаков, и кончил еще несчастливее».[73]

> One of those who was most loved by comrades, with a light sense, a clean soul, he had almost the same merits, as Esakov, and finished still unfortunately.

Others noted that Pouschine's collegial disposition in exile reflected many of the progressive intentions of the Lyceum. As the Decembrist N. V. Basargin characterized Pouschine's enlightened disposition:

> «Всем сердцем любил свою родину, но без фанатизма. Основательно знал отечественную литературу, правильно, даже красиво говорил и писал по-русски. Патриотизм его был истинный, просвещенный, вызывал симпатию и уважение. По своим взглядам он был выше всех своих товарищей».[74]

> With the whole of his heart, he loved his country, but without fantasy. He thoroughly knew the native literature, correctly, and even wrote and spoke Russian beautifully. His patriotism was sincere, enlightened, sympathetic, and respectful. By these views he was higher than all his comrades.

Pouschine retained like-mindedness with Lyceum classmates during both his school days and his exile; throughout both periods he received praise for his righteous disposition. He exemplified the school's progressive nature through his patriotic devotion to ameliorating Russia's cultural life.

As the Lyceum alumni pursued different careers, contrasting life experiences began to eviscerate their mutual, personal understanding of one another. The group attained broad influence in society. Alumni became military leaders, government figures, artists, and even, in one case, an adventurer. Pouschine and Pushkin aptly exhibited the two primary means graduates pursued to promote progress Russia: the political and the artistic. While their differing outlooks did not hinder their friendship, they did impede a sense of like-mindedness that weakened the Lyceum group as an emotional community. Pouschine wrote in his memoirs:

> «Находясь в постоянной дружбе с Пушкиным, мы разно смотрели на людей и на вещи и постоянно высказывали свои разногласия».[75]
>
> Being in constant friendship with Pushkin, we saw people and things differently and we constantly expressed our differences.

This sense of "express[ion]" indicated an emotional difference in the two men's attitudes. Some students, like Pushkin, focused on artistic endeavors, involving themselves in literary circles in St. Petersburg. Many of them became writers and poets and distinguished themselves by their "prankish" spirit.[76] Their discussions were unique in their propensity for lewd or taboo topics, such as sexuality, flirtation, and playfulness. Other students, including Pouschine, got involved in secret societies dedicated to political change in Russia. Lyceum alumni involved in revolutionary groups were characterized by earnest and humble attitudes, though

Lyceum men were generally united by their commitment to raising the community's spirit through arousing interest in a more culturally rich Russia.

The Lyceum group differed from the political Decembrists in that they were able to intertwine their desires for noble friendship and cultural advancement. While the Decembrists often cited their individual labor, the Lyceum group viewed cultural improvement as a collective effort. Accordingly, even in exile, Pouschine depended on his relationships with Lyceum friends to advance intellectual life in Siberia. In their spare time, the exiled Lyceum men often read scholarly journals, discussed literature, or criticized other writers to stimulate intellectual discourse. Moreover, the Lyceum's former director Y. A. Engel'gart provided Pouschine with reading material and encouraged him to write his memoir, *Notes on Pushkin*.[77] Former Lyceum classmates even arranged for a piano to be sent to Pouschine in Yalutorovsk so that his daughter could learn to play.

In exile, Pouschine found emotional relief in his Lyceum friendships thanks to their ability to provide him elating memories and sentiments. Throughout his sentence, Pouschine's interest in his Lyceum classmates did not wane. He wrote to his classmate I. V. Malinovsky:

> «Связь моя со всеми товарищами Лицея нисколько не ослаблена временем; пусть она в них сохранится в той же свежести».[78]
>
> My connection with all Lyceum friends did not at all weaken with time; may it be preserved in them with the same freshness.

Pouschine felt strong loyalty to his former classmates, and even affirmed hope for the attachment to continue. He thus confirmed the high value of these connections for him. In addition to such tender compassion, Pouschine also benefited from the material aid of Lyceum friendships.

Through Malinovsky, he received funds and an introduction to Prince S. G. Volkonsky, a fellow Decembrist exiled to Siberia, to help aid his settlement in Yalutorovsk.

A particularly poignant act of Lyceum support came in 1852, when Pouschine received from his classmate F. F. Matyushkin a piano for his daughter, Annushka. The gift of the piano exemplified the Lyceum spirit as it engaged existing friendships in promoting cultural development – in this case, by bringing music to Siberia.

As a student at the Lyceum, Matyushkin was well liked by both students and educators, and was especially noted for his dedication to his academic interests. From a young age, he was truly passionate about the sea – far more than he was about any other topic. After graduation, he joined the Russian navy and participated in numerous legendary sea voyages, including a circumnavigation of the world.[79] While his expertise gave key insight into naval reforms, and his name was proposed as someone who should join the Decembrist cause, Matyushkin did not participate in the uprising.[80]

Matyushkin reflected the values of the Lyceum friendship, rather than the values of a Decembrist or family member, given his enthusiastic devotion to cultural advancement. The tone of the letters amply showcased the Lyceum spirit with a jovial and enthusiastic outlook on reviving school memories. Through a robust correspondence, he and Pouschine reunited over their interest in improving Russian culture. Pouschine himself celebrated the Lyceum's bountiful, elating atmosphere, exclaiming:

«Одним словом, ура Лицею старого чекана»![81]
In a word, hurrah for the Lyceum's old coinage!

Lyceum Emotion: Exuberance

In his letters with Matyushkin from 1852 and 1853, Pouschine expressed an exuberance for his relationships with his old schoolmates, an abundant joy from reviving nostalgic memories to advance cultural life in Siberia. Pouschine displayed his emotions outwardly with a copious amount of exclamatory phrases.

While the Decembrist relationships were based on a continuing advocacy of auspicious civic advancement, the Lyceum friendships were based more on a shared attachment to youthful memories. In his letters to classmates, Pouschine's exuberance came from both his joy for their lasting friendships and from his hope of strengthening his own personal spirit. He proved meaningfully comforted by confirming the Lyceum friendships' devotion to advancing Russian culture. In their letters, the Lyceum classmates bonded over society's sensatory and artistic experiences. While the Decembrists positioned friendships as a means of political transformation, Pouschine relied on Lyceum friendships for their emotional support, aiming to revive his youthful delight in himself and his surroundings.

The letters between Pouschine and Matyushkin reveal that mementos from their Lyceum days were a beloved source of joy for them. For example, the classmates' portraits, gifted piano, and the Lyceum song bestowed a sense of elation by providing external validation of Pouschine's cherished memories. Pouschine clearly found great meaning in these artifacts of his Lyceum days and thought it important to preserve them. He ascribed a similar purpose to the letters themselves, and letters from classmates revived such pleasant memories in Matyushkin, for one, as well. The resulting tone was highly nostalgic; Pouschine aimed to gladden Matyushkin by reminiscing about their blissful, youthful moments. Pouschine evoked the power of an artistic emblem to reawaken his gratifying feelings; he confirmed that even past joy can arouse present elation.

Ultimately, Pouschine used his own sense of elation to bolster the broader spirit of his community. First, he referred to Matyushkin's portrait to describe the reawakening of a sentimental friendship within himself, as such nostalgic encounters prompted comforting reminiscence. Pouschine initially presented his nostalgic reaction to the portrait:

> «Разумеется, я бы тебя не узнал, но узнаю твое прежнее сердце».[82]
> Of course, but I would not recognize you, but I would recognize your old heart.

Pouschine underscored the tenderness of his friendship with Matyushkin, in sharp contrast to the pragmatism in his friendships with Decembrists. Pouschine suggested that their relationship transcended the current circumstances. Although he would not be able to "recognize" his old friend were they to see each other again, their friendship still existed deeply within the "old heart." The heart represented his old friend metonymically to underscore their fondness for each other. Such an image thus bolstered the romantic nature of the Lyceum friendships: the friends were brought together idyllically by heartfelt sentiments. Pouschine deepened his connection to the portrait by describing his own reaction to the image:

> «Часто гляжу на твой портрет–тут мысли перебегают все десятки лет нашей разлуки».[83]
> Often I look at your portrait–then thoughts run across all the tens of years of our separation.

Pouschine positioned the portrait itself as a means of preserving these internal bonds of friendship. The "tens of years of separation" indeed acknowledged the friends' distance, one that was unlikely to be overcome by any personal meeting. Yet the portrait still appeared to provide pleasure, given that Pouschine looked upon it "often," while his memories took an agency as they "run across" his active and powerful mind. Pouschine's description of the portrait kept the friendship alive by presenting a real connection in both the heart and mind. Pouschine exhibited sentimental fulfillment by reminiscing on his friendship, thus positioning it as a source of abundant pleasure and emotional comfort.

Second, Pouschine displayed the amiable purpose of these relationships by describing how the comfort he received from them produced an overwhelming joy that could be shared. He exhibited an outpouring of excitement for this confirmation of the Lyceum friendship, describing his enthusiasm upon receiving the piano for his daughter and confirming his continued rapture as he struggled to express his emotions in words:

> «Отрадное чувство мое вам понятно без лишних возгласов, потому что вы, действуя так любезно, заставляете меня забывать скучные расчеты в деле дружбы».[84]
>
> My comforting feeling is clear to you without unnecessary exclamations, because you, acting so kindly, compel me to forget boring calculations in the realm of friendship.

Pouschine underscored the ethereal nature of Lyceum joy. Formal, external measures of friendship – "exclamations" and "calculations" – are "unnecessary." Instead, he celebrated the "pleasant emotion" imparted by kind action. His "clear" and elating sensation did not require validation by social convention. Such a romantic, idealistic attitude underscored the emotive purpose of friendship: friends prove their connection by arousing joy in one another. Accordingly, Pouschine presumed that this gift elated Matyushkin as well:

> «Принимаю ваш подарок с тем же чувством, с которым вы его послали мне, далекому».[85]
> I accept your gift with the same feeling with which you sent it to me, from far away.

Thus, in addition to the physical objects that connect the friends, Pouschine looks to emotions for further unity. He experiences "the same feeling" as Matyushkin, establishing a moment of mutual bliss between friends. This reciprocity displays the friends' emotional understanding of one another, even across significant distances, as it occurs from "from far away." In this way above all, the correspondence between Pouschine and Matyushkin demonstrated their sustained connection to the Lyceum's emotional community.

Finally, Pouschine established the purposeful effect of his Lyceum memories on his own disposition by revealing their power to ameliorate his spirit mystically. In addition to describing how these relationships provided him with rapture, he demonstrated how such exuberance could meaningfully improve his general outlook. He described the strength of friendship in reference to the piano gift, which rose to vivid, comforting thoughts that imitate physical proximity:

> «Если бы вы знали, как все это живо перенесло меня в ваш круг».[86]
> If you knew how this all vividly moved me into your sphere.

Pouschine wrote this remark after opening and observing the piano; it highlighted how the activity strengthened his sensation of connection to Matyushkin, as he felt moved "into his sphere." Pouschine's writing indicated that in addition to the physical connection established by the transfer of this piano, the men themselves were brought together by a sustained mystical connection.

In addition to discussing the strengthened perception of friendship, Pouschine also described how the Lyceum friendships benefited him individually as they bolstered his will to live on in exile:

> «Отпустить шутку случается и теперь–слава богу, иначе нельзя бы так долго прожить на горизонте не совсем светлом».[87]
>
> [My mind] happened to release this joke, now – thank God, otherwise it would be impossible to live so long on a horizon that is not quite light.

Pouschine noted his appreciation for his gladdening memories. He presented them lightheartedly, as "joke[s]," noting their capricious nature. Yet the surprising recollections nonetheless inspired in him a will to live despite such bleak conditions. Their miraculous power was insinuated as Pouschine thanked "God" for his comforting reminiscences. While Pouschine indicated the inconstancy of the Lyceum friendships, he praised their ongoing ability to provide motivating joy during his period of personal hardship. Pouschine thus revealed a broad, spiritual power within these friendships for overcoming his suffering.

Pouschine used his letters to attest to his sincere appreciation for the Lyceum friendships. This opportunity to reconnect with his former comrades and share joyous moments inspired great exuberance in the exiled prisoner. In his letters, he indicated that his connection to his Lyceum friends aroused fond feelings, and he also praised the Lyceum's ability to elate his general spirit. Ultimately, both these benefits provided Pouschine with sentimental pleasure. In contrast to the austere and reliable connections with the Decembrists, however, Pouschine's friendships with

Lyceum classmates were less constant. In his writings, he acknowledged the ease at which he can lose touch with old friends, and that the friends themselves could lack a sense of mutual understanding. Yet, throughout the correspondence of Pouschine and Matyushkin, Pouschine demonstrated the numerous ways in which their shared Lyceum spirit had become meaningfully revived. Lyceum friendships thus proved remarkable for their ability to provide pleasure to a distant community, despite that community's physical and emotional removal from Siberian life.

Lyceum "Style"

Pouschine captured the Lyceum community's jovial character in his letters by indulging in more lyrical language than he did with the Decembrists. Rather than describing the letters' general style, this section will focus on Pouschine's most noteworthy stylistic choice: quoting lyrics in his letters. These inclusions prove intriguing, for they transcended everyday, mundane language. Although the words are not his own, Pouschine used lyrics to express his emotions. The two main artistic works to which Pouschine referred – the Lyceum's "National Song" and Pushkin's "In the Depths of Siberian Mines" – both conveyed the compassion inherent in Lyceum friendships. Their sentimental messages depicted Lyceum friendships with romantic heroism and idealism. The two works differ in tone: the Lyceum song is a comic, playful display of camaraderie between friends, and the poem is formal, lyric verse composed by Pushkin once he was an established writer. Nevertheless, they inspired nostalgia for past friendships, and ultimately enabled Pouschine to convey upsetting emotions in an affectionate manner. As his lyric references became more solemn, the lyrics themselves spoke to an increasingly wide audience. Pouschine thus personalized joyful feelings while generalizing distress.

Pouschine evoked the Lyceum's "National Song" to revive memories of himself in Matyushkin's mind, thus celebrating their own lasting friendship. While expressing gratitude for the piano sent for his daughter, Pouschine used the collegial song to recall his Lyceum class, thereby reawakening his joyous friendship with Matyushkin:

> «Большой Jeannot / Мильон bon mots / Без умыслу проворит».[88]
>
> Great Jeannot / a million witty remarks / Will speak without slyness.

Pouschine used the class's traditional song to include the Lyceum spirit. He quoted its verses about himself to identify as a coherent member of the group.

The lyrics further displayed his lasting loyalty to the Lyceum. He wrote selected words in French to evoke the school's learned, refined nature. Ironically, these references also show Pouschine's high regard for the French Enlightenment–the very ideas that inspired the actions that led to his exile–which was sparked in his Lyceum studies. Nonetheless, the use of French indicated his lasting adherence to the Lyceum's progressive spirit and devotion to his own revolutionary ideas. Beyond these serious implications, the song was playful. Pouschine referred to himself by his boyhood nickname, "the Great Jeannot," to portray himself intimately. Furthermore, his tease, "a million witty remarks / will speak without slyness," commented on Pouschine's own use of language. The couplet denoted his magnanimous character, suggesting honorable intentions in reaching out to his friend. Pouschine used this bit of playful song to exhibit the continued existence of his boyhood self; he remained committed to

Lyceum ideals despite grueling exile.

Pouschine also used lyrics to represent the Lyceum group by glorifying their joyful past unity. He addressed the Lyceum group's tragic hardships–the deaths of two members of their class–by reminiscing on their group's past joy:

> «Где Броглио, где Тырков? Помогли Тыркову черти: / Он везде нуль и четвертый»![89]
>
> Where is Broglio? Where is Tyrkov? Devils helped Tyrkov:? He is forever lost to us!

Pouschine's evocations spoke to art's given ability to preserve these departed men's spirits; the song serves to revive their spirits in the minds of the surviving friends. At the Lyceum, the song had an intimate, unifying role: the boys sang it together, typically away from their teachers.[90] The song thus bolstered their sense of emotional community, as it fulfilled the boys' desire for establishing a humorous, lighthearted, and festive atmosphere.[91] Reviving these lyrics from the song thus paid tribute to the broader group of Lyceum classmates and reflected their ongoing regard for the collective group. Pouschine thus acknowledged the physical decay of the Lyceum class–through the reference to deceased classmates–yet refrained from somber language to reflect on such tragedies. It portrayed the Lyceum group as an emotional community and conserved a shared *esprit de corps* through its memorialization of joyous friendships.

Pouschine's reference to Pushkin's poem expressed thanks for the Lyceum group's sympathy for its exiled classmates. Pushkin's verse depicted intimate concern among dear friends. Pouschine confirmed his appreciation for the poem by requesting a physical copy:

> «Когда-нибудь надобно тебе прислать послание к нам

всем: Во глубине сибирских руд / Храните гордое терпенье – и пр».[92]

Sometime, you need to send a letter to us all: "In the depths of the Siberian ore / Maintain your proud endurance – and so on.

In referring this poem, Pouschine appeals to the lasting connection between Lyceum classmates and the exiled Decembrists among them. Its majestic tone can appeal to a broad audience – past, present, and future alike – by sharing Pushkin's glorious outlook on the Decembrists. He praised their "proud endurance," and invoked martyred image of them. This forlorn acknowledgement of the Decembrists' personal suffering in exile reflected the lasting strength of the emotional ties of Lyceum graduates. The poem, however, wavered between two registers – grand, poetic language and private displays of friendship. For example, the introduction «во глубине» (typically, «в глубине» would be said) was used to "create the expectation" of a high, poetic style.[93] However, this formality juxtaposed the intimacy of the second line, which references a song written by Delvig for the Lyceum graduation.[94]

Just as Pushkin displayed his value of Lyceum friendships in his intimate references, Pouschine affirmed his adherence to Lyceum ideals through his strong appreciation the poem. His reference to such somber themes in his letter allowed Pouschine to display greater emotional intimacy with Matyushkin, as he opened up by describing his own struggles in exile.

Pouschine's lyric style connected his letters to the high artistic interests of the Lyceum. He initially aroused the jovial, intellectual Lyceum spirit by playfully incorporating artistic language into his conversational letters. However, the references themselves became increasingly somber as Pouschine used lyrics that discussed increasingly weighty themes. The references evolved from lighthearted school jokes to formal, solemn literature and allowed Pouschine to strengthen his emotional connection to Matyushkin over the course of this correspondence. While he began the correspondence with reminiscences of happy memories, he ultimately retreated to the grief of exile.

Lyceum Content

The Lyceum letters primarily discussed the arrival of the piano to Siberia: Pouschine revealed that this event provided him with a sense of purpose as it allowed him to bolster artistic pursuits throughout the community. Pouschine portrayed the exuberant atmosphere prompted by the new piano. He included Matyushkin alongside the slow process of uncovering it, imparting the festive spirit on the former classmate. Pouschine repeatedly infused the jovial, Lyceum spirit; he praised the school itself, the director, and his memories, framing its beneficial purpose in his present life. The grandeur of the piano implied the beauty of the original Lyceum spirit.

Pouschine attained personal fulfillment from enjoying the piano himself and sharing it with others. His praise of the piano evolved from emotional to functional over time. He demonstrated that his initial joy had recognizable beneficial repercussions on the community. Just as Pouschine emotionally reawakened his friendship with Matyushkin in order to improve his personal attitude, he portrayed how this active reawakening of the Lyceum spirit helped advance cultural life in Siberia.

Pouschine established the piano as an emblem of the Lyceum, likening its purpose to the Lyceum's progressive intentions. He underscored the strong connection between this piano and Lyceum memories:

> «Фортепиано в Сибири будет известно под именем лицейского; и теперь всем слушающим и понимающим высказываю то, что отрадно срывается с языка. Аннушка вместе с музыкой будет на нем учиться знать и любить старый Лицей»![95]

> The piano in Siberia will be known under the name of the Lyceum; Now, I am overjoyed to tell to all you who listen and understand what I can not hold back anymore and cannot express in language. Annushka, together with our music, on it will learn to know and love our old Lyceum!

By naming the piano "Lyceum," Pouschine made it into a symbol of the cherished school. Accordingly, Pouschine framed its purpose to perpetuate the Lyceum spirit. He first described its elating effect on his daughter, confirming that Annushka will "learn to know and love the old Lyceum!" The emotional verb to "love" indicated that the piano would influence others' emotions, as well as spread awareness. Pouschine thus presented the piano as a tool for "expres[sion]": it would emulate the jovial, Lyceum spirit, thereby emotionally uplifting others through "the music." The piano offered the opportunity to impart an enlightening sensation on the Siberians, just as the Lyceum enlightened the students with Western intellectual works. This emotional sensibility suggested that the piano was capable of expanding the Lyceum emotional community by reviving the school's progressive and patriotic spirit. Pouschine thus kept the Lyceum spirit alive as his exiled community now experienced the collegial sentiment.

After opening the piano, Pouschine offered insight into its effect on the community by citing its ability to engage those who encounter it. Pouschine first described how the piano enchanted others, as its beautiful sounds inspired amazement:

> «Подняли крышку, и все ахнули от восхищения... Тронула Аннушка первая клавиши, и представь себе, что все звуки верны...Все вы явились около меня, всех вас я целовал, обнимал».[96]

> They lifted the lid and everyone gasped from admiration... Annushka touched the first keys, and imagine that all the sounds are correct...All of you appeared around me, all of you I kissed, embraced.

The piano enchanted the community with its majestic presence. The viewers initially reacted physically, as they "gasp with admiration." Annushka "touched the first keys," demonstrating her curiosity of the instrument. Pouschine described his own response to the piano more intimately: "all of you appeared near me, all of you I kissed, embraced." Through conjuring past memories, the piano responded to Pouschine's loneliness. He expressed the pleasure from validation of friendship, as he imagined affectionately "kiss[ing]" and "embrac[ing]" his friends. This sensation of reunion thus demonstrated the piano's ability to amuse the solitary man.

Finally, Pouschine explained the piano's novelty to underscore its position in the community, as it prompted excitement for enhanced artistic life. He asserted the functional superiority of the Lyceum piano compared to other instruments in Siberia:

> «Ваше фортепиано–первое в нашем городке– это не много еще значит, хотя, прочем, здесь до него было уже пять инструментов; не во всяком уездном городке, особенно сибирском, встречается такое богатство музыкальное».[97]

> Your grand piano is the first in our town–its arrival should not mean much, because there were already five instruments before it; but not in every provincial town, especially Siberian, can one find such musical wealth.

Pouschine praised the piano as a "musical treasure." Compared to the ethereal nature of the revived memories, the measurable "wealth" conveyed recognizable, objective value. He compared this Lyceum piano to the "five instruments before it." Yet this piano's impressiveness enabled Pouschine to anticipate cultural advancement. He further underscored its originality by stating that such a piano is found "not in every chief town, especially Siberian." Pouschine accordingly validated Matyushkin's gift as an item of value for the settlement. Pouschine thus celebrated Matyushkin and the Lyceum's ability to have a clear, positive influence on the intellectual opportunities of those in Siberia by acting upon the community's shared desire to rectify Russia's backwardness.

Ultimately, Pouschine's letters described the piano's enchanting air. In his letters, Pouschine introduces the piano as a physical emblem of the Lyceum. Although he initially associated the piano with memories of his youthful joy, Pouschine recognized that it transmitted jovial sentiment. Its ability to influence other's emotions indicated a sense of expansion for the Lyceum emotional community. Pouschine explained the piano's ability to entrance the community by inspiring a sense of admiration and reminiscence through its association with fond memories of a bygone time. In the letters, it attained a mystical and captivating power over both himself and unfamiliar onlookers while benefitting Siberia functionally.

Conclusion

The Lyceum group cohered as a distinct emotional community, bound by its common interests in the artistic and emotional advancement of Russia. Although Lyceum graduates worked to improve Russia in a variety of ways – politically, artistically, and militarily – they were united by their shared educational experience. The Lyceum intended to inspire patriotic commitment in its students, but it simultaneously catalyzed their sentimental commitment to one another. Even though differing interests, careers, and life trajectories undermined the men's ability to understand each other sympathetically, the classmates nonetheless supported each other throughout their lives. And while at times this support was financial, members of the Lyceum group focused their attention on the emotional benefits of friendship. The emotional community stayed intact because its members derived pleasure from recalling joyous Lyceum memories; as a result, the community occupied itself with spreading such joyous sentiments throughout society.

The piano gift embodied the joyful character of the Lyceum group through its impressive ability to transmit their high spirits throughout Russia. In the correspondence, Pouschine noted that the piano provided much pleasure for him and to the larger community. He portrayed the gift as a means of reviving and perpetuating the cherished, Lyceum atmosphere. By incorporating lyrics into his words, Pouschine deepened his relationship with Matyushkin by harnessing art's ability to affect readers emotionally. The works he cited addressed increasingly broad audiences, but they shared intimate references to the school days. Pouschine also appeared to be gratified by his ability to harness the goal of spreading cheer among the classmates. His descriptions depicted the beauty of the Lyceum spirit by describing this majestic air that the Lyceum piano could bestow upon all of Siberia.

The Lyceum emotional community was distinct in its interest in perpetuating the Lyceum spirit, which its members treated as a treasure. By teaching his daughter to play the songs and to "love" the Lyceum, Pouschine imparted the Lyceum's culture to both distant Siberia and the next generation. In his letters, Pouschine noted his use of portraits and other artifacts (such as copies of Pushkin's poems) to preserve happy memories of his Lyceum friendships. While the Decembrist and family emotional communities evolved to suit changing circumstances, Lyceum alumni stayed loyal to one another despite changing life circumstances. The correspondence revealed the ties between sentiment and tradition, as appeals to past joy reawaken unyielding pleasure.

Chapter III: Family

Annushka's Carriage

Family Background

The correspondence between Ivan Pouschine and his family revealed that the Pouschines placed a great emphasis on the spiritual well-being of others. This focus on personal, soulful stability fostered highly intimate and open relations between correspondents. The Decembrists and the Lyceum group were unified by likeminded outlooks shaped by experience, but family members were united by birth, and not necessarily by any shared vision. The Pouschine family constituted an emotional community given its members' common desire to protect the personal well-being of family members and dear friends.

Although other Pouschine family members were part of this community, this chapter will focus on three individuals: Ivan, his brother Nikolai, and his daughter Annushka. While other groups sought recognizable influence within the community, the Pouschines relied on correspondence to attain the personal gratification that enabled righteous action. They shared a desire to support one another emotionally, with the goal of ultimately ensuring that each is capable of serving society. This intimate, spiritual support proved especially strong during moments of hardship, and inspired the individuals to abide by righteous values in emotionally strenuous moments. Pouschine's letters thus showed his abundant appreciation for these connections with family members as they enabled him to attain personal, soulful solace.

Throughout his life, Ivan easily maintained friendly relations with others thanks to his amiable character. His familial relations were often inhibited by his life choices, however, and separated him from his family. For example, attending the Lyceum, taking a post in a low Moscow court, and participating in the daring Decembrist uprising all took Ivan away from home, both physically and spiritually. Family relations endured during his exile despite the physical and social distance that existed between Ivan and his family.

In correspondence with his family, Ivan discussed one decision that distanced him from a family member: sending his daughter away to St. Petersburg to establish her professionally. Writing about her departure to his brother Nikolai, Ivan exhibited his altruistic selflessness. Annushka was one of his few sources of company in Siberia; however, she stood to benefit professionally from the opportunity in St. Petersburg. In the letter, he maintained a humble yet cheerful attitude towards the loss of his daughter's presence, positioning his family as a network of emotional, and often physical, care that helped him overcome the emotional hardships of solitude.

Pouschine's letters to his family revealed Ivan at his most intimate: he relied on these connections to discuss personal struggles. In contrast to the interest in social matters expressed in the correspondence between Pouschine and the Decembrist and Lyceum groups, these letters addressed the emotional well–being of individuals. Letters to family delved into a variety of intimate topics: tragic loss, social transgressions, terminal illness, and even profound familial love. His heartfelt openness when discussing these intimate topics provided insight into Ivan's personal concerns, regarding both his own emotional standing and the well–being of others. The taboo nature of much of the content inscribed his letters with sincerity. For example, he described an old woman's illness graphically and introduced acquaintances frankly, rather than crafting careful, polite phrases. This openness of expression thus marked the letters with deep intimacy, as Ivan presented his views with minimal inhibitions.

These deeply intimate bonds were remarkable given Ivan's history of disquieting family relations. For the majority of his life, Ivan lived independently from his kin. He left home in 1811, at the age of thirteen, to attend the Tsarskoye Selo Lyceum, and did not marry until 1857, at age fifty-nine. He fathered and raised two illegitimate children, yet sent both away before their maturity.[98] These strained relationships began in his early childhood. Until he was eleven, he lived on the family estate in Marino, in the Bronnitsy district outside of Moscow, with his parents and ten siblings. Ivan's mother, A. M. Pouschine, originally of the wealthy Ryabinin family, was unable to manage the estate due to mental illness.[99] His strict father, I. P. Pouschine, was a lieutenant-general, fleet general-merchant, and senator. The children suffered at the hands of these two parents: the father struggled to provide financially, and the mother's mental illness had a harsh emotional effect on the young children.[100]

Pouschine's childhood suffered in the face of ambiguous authority and general disarray. His younger brother Mikhail described the disorder of the Pouschine household in their early childhood, noting the lack of familial unity due to discordant relations:

«Из воспоминаний детства более всего внедрились в

память серьезность отца, помешательство матери, начальство старших сестер, отсутствие всякого присмотра со стороны гувернеров Трините, Вранкена, Троппе и других, баловство старой, любимой няни Авдотьи Степановны и при ней дружба с горничными».[101]

From my childhood recollections, the ones most embedded in my memory are my father's sternness; my mother's insanity; the superiority of the older sisters; the absence of any supervision from the tutors Trinité, Vrankena, Troppe, and others; the pampering of the old, beloved nanny Advotya Stepanova and friendship with the maids during her time.

Mikhail related the culture of unreliability throughout the Pouschine family, given the ambiguous supervision. No member of the household appeared to express concern for the emotional well–being of the children, which stood in contrast to the intimacy apparent in Ivan's later correspondence with Nikolai. Further, the lack of empathy in Ivan's parents juxtaposed sharply with his empathy for Annushka.

In exile, Pouschine was outspoken about his conservative opinions on family life. He disavowed interclass marriages for the Decembrists. He believed that families ought to be cohesive units; accordingly, he disapproved of relations between Decembrists and native Siberians. He pessimistically commented on the Decembrist Prince E. P. Obolensky's wedding to a Siberian nurse:

«Невольным образом, глядя на них, вспоминаю курицу, которая высидела утенка и бегает по берегу, когда тот плавает. Кажется, вообще мало может быть симпатии: и лета, и понятия, и привычки, и связи–все разное».[102]

Involuntarily, looking at them, I recall a chicken who laid a duckling and ran along the shore when he was swimming. It seems, in general there could be little sympathy: the years, concepts, habits, and connections – everything is different.

Pouschine's emphasis on the differences between individuals – the "years, concepts, habits, connections" – revealed his high esteem for the family unity. He framed the family as a source of mutual understanding and sympathy, suggesting that strong alliances depend on similar social standing. While Ivan dramatized the social differences in the couple by likening them to separate animals, he acknowledged that the underlying issue remained emotional: the lack of "sympathy" between the two individuals.

While Pouschine denounced intimate relations with Siberians, he himself had taboo affairs that resulted in illegitimate children, Annushka and Ivan. Pouschine hardly kept the children a secret; he adopted and raised them through childhood. He even requested that his Lyceum friends send him a piano so that Annushka could learn to play and sent his son to be raised by his brother Nikolai.

Although Pouschine expressed genuine warmth for his children and treated them with unwavering affection, their illegitimate status incurred a need for privacy.[103] For example, out of tact, Pouschine kept the identity of their mothers largely secret (though he eventually revealed the identity of Ivan's mother, Drosida Ivanovna, the widow of Decembrist V. K. Kiukhelbeker, to few close friends.)[104] He even arranged for her to live in privacy outside the city throughout her pregnancy to hide the dishonorable situation.[105] While his children were undeniably dear to Ivan, their precarious position as illegitimate contributed to the complexity of his family life.

In the midst of such unconventional family relationships,

however, Ivan's brother Nikolai provided unyielding, poignant support that enabled Ivan to express deep concern for others' emotions. Little is known about Nikolai Ivanovich Pouschine. He was an official based in St. Petersburg and appeared devoted to his family. He reportedly lived in the capital with his wife, Mariia, and had two daughters, Maria and Olga.[106] He later adopted and raised Ivan's extramarital son, Ivan. Nikolai had long displayed deep loyalty to his brother. Most remarkably, in 1842, Nikolai obtained permission to live in Siberia, rented a house near his brother in Tobolsk, and began carrying out repairs himself.[107]

Nikolai's behavior was a good representation of how Pouschine family members tended to relate to one another, as he was outside the Decembrists and Lyceum communities. Nikolai had no association with the Lyceum group, nor any personal involvement with the Decembrists. Further, he had no clear political alliances, and neither faced exile nor participated in military campaigns.

Correspondence between the two brothers shows that Pouschine regarded Nikolai as an educated, intellectual man concerned with family life. Ivan's communication with Nikolai was both emotional and practical. Ivan regularly professed his love and appreciation for his brother using deeply affectionate language. But he also dedicated much attention to resolving rudimentary domestic affairs – transporting books, sorting accommodation for traveling friends, and reporting updates from others. In comparing Pouschine's correspondence with family members to his correspondence with the Decembrists and the Lyceum friends, one sees that with family members, Pouschine made requests more casually and used affectionate language more liberally, indicating a heightened degree of intimacy. Unlike his letters to the Decembrists,

Pouschine's family letters contained no political discourse; they instead focused on personal problems.

In contrast to the tone Pouschine employed in his Lyceum group letters, his tone in family letters was practical and lacked sentimental flourish and artistic references. The family letters highlighted Ivan's sincere sympathy for the emotional standing of singular individuals. The Decembrist and Lyceum group letters paid tribute to the noble cause of friendship.[108] In family correspondence, however, Pouschine displayed the value of brotherhood. He appeared to consider a brother to be a source of sympathy rather than someone with whom he could discuss progressive action. The familial relationship was thus marked by a heightened fidelity due to the deeply intimate cause of their relationship: providing emotional support emboldened others to carry out meaningful action.

Family Emotion: Appreciation

In his letters to Nikolai, Ivan distinguished himself by expressing an abundance of appreciation. He exhibited a high regard for his family through ceaseless professions of empathy for his brother and other dear friends. Appreciation came as a grateful response to supportive concern for one another's emotional hardships. While the Decembrists shared an interest in political reform, and the Lyceum group bonded over shared memories, Ivan sustained his familial relationship by appreciating his brother's unrelenting support for his soulful comfort. The brothers' relations inspired spiritual consolation by confirming the emotional benefits of their service to others and the community. Nikolai aided Ivan in a variety of ways, including providing intellectual stimulation by sending reading materials, offering physical care when hosting Ivan's friend, supplying practical goods such as clothing, and extending spiritual kinship on holidays. The multifaceted understanding between the brothers resulted in a strong bond that facilitated a mystical and emotional connection. They were able to experience each other's elating stories, receive consolation in response to tragedy, and even develop profound solace through reminiscences. While the discussion in their correspondence spanned a wide variety of themes, a consistent motif is Ivan's gratitude for the soulful support he received from his brother.

This intimate gratitude between the brothers was distinct, for it focused on the well-being of individuals, rather than on the general status of the larger community. Intimate brotherhood was rooted in the private sphere, given their mutual interest in supporting each other emotionally. Rather than striving to advance public ambitions – such as politics or art – these familial interactions served to resolve personal troubles. For example, Ivan once refused to discuss politics because the subject made him "unhappy." Instead, the Pouschines relied on each other when confronting emotional hardship, their emotional connection ranging from bestowing elation to easing troubling grief. Just like the Decembrists and the Lyceum group, Ivan's pursuit of gratitude called the brothers to noble action by bettering one other's soulful standing.

Ivan initially registered emotional comfort from Nikolai by expressing elation while reading the correspondence. Through his letters, Pouschine lived vicariously through Nikolai: he transcended his Siberian despondency through stories of St. Petersburg festivities:

> «Вы просто делаете чудеса, добрый Николай Иванович, все на балах самых церемонных. Я просто посмеялся, читая ваш рассказ об этих похождениях».[109]

You just do wonders, dear Nikolai Ivanovich, at all the most ceremonial balls. I simply laughed, reading your story about these antics.

Pouschine positioned Nikolai's letters as a form of entertainment, as they provided a sense of "adventure" and "laugh[ter.]"

The exciting, humorous event – the "ceremonial" ball – stood in contrast to the purposeful, consequential activities discussed with the Decembrists. However, such an anecdote still filled Ivan with pleasure. He confirmed his emotional connection to his brother's story as it brought him to "laugh." This impulsive response indicated that Pouschine was recognizably cheered by the story. Further, the expression "you do just wonders" affirmed that the story amply captured Ivan's curiosity. His escapist pleasure from reading the story – becoming absorbed in his brother's social outings – revealed the possibility for elation from conceiving another's life in a distant society.

In addition to providing the brothers with a vehicle to share elating sentiments, the letters also enabled them to commiserate over tragic circumstance together. Receiving news of a cousin severly wounded in war, Ivan offered consolation by using his emotional intimacy to mimic physical intimacy:

> «Правду вы говорите, что мильон лет ко мне не писали, поэтому и я как-то давно с вами молча, но это не мешало мне мысленно часто бывать в вашем домашнем кругу–в уединенном вашем предместье. Молча делил с вами и с Николаем тяжелые ощущения, которых у нас было много с тех пор, как мы не писали друг другу. Очень верю, что вам тяжело было вести речь о том, что каждый из нас читал в печатных столбцах».[110]

You are right to say that for a million years they have not written to me, and so I somehow long ago became silent with you, but this does not impede me from often being with your home circle in spirit -- in your secluded region. I silently shared with you and with Nikolai heavy relations, of which we have had many since we last write one another. I very much believe, that it was hard for you to discuss that each of us read in printed columns.

The brothers proved their ability to console each other in times of tragedy. Ivan presented their ability to confront personal hardship together. They rely on one another, as they "share" "heavy relations," indicating that the brothers served to ease each other's sadness. He also mimicked their physical connection, positioning himself "in [Nikolai's] home circle" to indicate that their connection could overcome geographic distance. These two means of fraternal connection underscored a fraternal purpose of offering support during times of suffering. Yet Ivan acknowledged the limitations of written correspondence by noting, "it was hard for you to talk about." He indicated that the brother's sympathy extended beyond mere words on a page. While the intellectual Lyceum group used poetry and literature to communicate profound ideas, the Pouschine brothers left the extent of their sympathy unstated. Nonetheless, their commiseration over tragedy evoked a consoling effect.

Ivan intensified his relationship with Nikolai with references to the broader spiritual sense of consolation established through their soulful connection. In celebrating his name's day, Ivan underscored the power of his emotional perception of Nikolai by describing the gratification he attained from imagined celebrations:

> «От души благодарю вас, что вспомнили мои майские дни. Я тоже 9-го числа был мысленно с вами, хотя мое поздравление не попало ко времени. Впрочем я надеюсь, что между нами эта хронология и без письменных проявлений всегда помниться и по-своему празднуется».[111]

From the soul I thank you, that you remembered my May Days. I also on the 9th was with you in spirit, although my congratulations did not get to you in time. Nevertheless, I hope that between us these days are without written displays and are always remembered and celebrated in their own way.

Ivan described the pleasure he took from considering mystical "spirit" interactions. He indicated the sincerity of his expression and depth of his memories by stating that he felt "from the soul." And this soulful sensation gave rise to invigorating gratitude, for both Nikolai's remembrance of May Day and for his own perception of connection. The celebration of "May Days" – or Ivan's name's day – were significant for religious reasons. The commemoration of a patron saint evoked the image of the Decembrists as martyrs, further eliciting Nikolai's familial sympathy. The reflection's emotionally beneficial outcome was indicated by Ivan's resulting "hope." He suggested, however, that such consideration trumped written correspondence: he preferred celebration to be "remembered" rather than confined to "written displays." Ivan's sense of reassurance appeared more meaningful in his own thoughts than could be indicated in words. He thus indicated his high regard for even a mere sensation of togetherness, which could connect the brothers in joyous celebration.

Ivan presented the culmination of familial support by writing Nikolai about attaining profound solace from God. Ivan displayed appreciation, similar to that for his brother, for the higher realm by describing the beneficial outcomes of submitting to God's will. He positioned himself as a "son of God" and celebrated divine comfort from his trust in Providence:

«Это просто благоволение свыше. Тут нечего

говорить эгоистически об разлуке. Явно Провидение благоволит, наше дело благодарить и благоговеть. И принимаю все это с глубокою благодарностию – проникнут этим отрадным чувством и точно не понимаю, за что так делается? Самый этот вопрос исполняет меня каким-то невыразимым внутренним, молитвенным утешением».[112]

This is simply a blessing from above. There is nothing egotistical to say about this separation. Clearly, Providence favors our decision to give gratitude and reverence. I accept all of this with deep adoration. To enter into these feelings of joy, and I do not quite understand, what caused all of this? This very question fills me with an inexpressible sense of personal, sacred comfort.

Ivan's relationship with God mirrors his connection with Nikolai as a source of solace. While Ivan used intimate interactions to attain comfort from Nikolai, he gained consolation from God passively. He showed deep humility by positioning God as the source of his "feelings of joy," indicating a lack of agency over his own spiritual peace. While Nikolai served to provide Ivan with fulfilling sympathy and pleasure, Ivan now discusses an even deeper sense of consolation – this "inexpressible sense of personal, sacred comfort" – that is governed by the spiritual realm. Ivan expounded on this divine connection with the repeated use of the Slavonic prefix «благо», instilling a spiritual tone in Ivan's language. The higher register of the prefix exhibited the sacredness of God's realm, contrasting the lower register of the words related to the earthly realm, such а «дело». Accordingly, even through language, Ivan portrayed a higher realm with profound significance that trumps his earthly dealings. While Ivan celebrated Nikolai's ability to provide comfort, he demonstrated the spiritual realm's ultimate power in bestowing true emotional solace.

Ivan's correspondence with Nikolai revealed his gratitude for soulful support in exile. His displays of thankfulness accompanied intimate moments in which he shared his emotions. The brothers supported each another with their ability to confront hardships together, and they gratified each other by transmitting elating emotions. The wide breadth of emotions discussed in the correspondence indicated the strength of the bond, as the brothers displayed a multi-faceted understanding of one another, ranging from practical aid to soulful understanding. The sincere depth of emotion enabled the brothers to display strong mutual sympathy for each other, even when they were unable to express their emotions coherently. As the emotions became more complex over the correspondence, Pouschine displayed how connection to the spiritual realm strengthened his resulting solace. Although Ivan ultimately indicated the supremacy of his connection to God's realm, he nonetheless used these intimate, fraternal bonds to discuss his profound appreciation for soulful consolation.

Family Style

Throughout his letters, Ivan's epistolary style reduced his own agency, resulting in a humble affect. This understated tone reflected his sense of appreciation for life by highlighting his regard for others. Pouschine minimized his own significance by portraying himself as unassuming and predominantly discussed the affairs of other family members and dear friends. According to Todd, members of the earlier Arzamasians group accentuated their own individuality by presenting themselves in correspondence with self-irony.[113] In contrast, Ivan typically refrained from using letters to express individuality; rather, he occupied himself with trying to understand the personal circumstances of others.

Pouschine's writing showed a deep concern to treat friendships with active engagement. His style developed, and then gratified, his brother Nikolai's interest in reflecting his own gratification from brotherly friendship. As his style emphasized the importance of others' activities over his own, he exhibited appreciation by accentuating the importance of family members and dear friends.

Ivan portrayed his own life unpretentiously by admitting the mundane and rudimentary nature of his habits. His modest affairs, such as regimented letter writing and repetitive meetings, contrasted with his intriguing reports on the arguably more interesting activities of others. Pouschine openly acknowledged the banality of his life, stating:

> «Я его к тебе не адресовал, потому что ничего нет занимательного».[114]
>
> I did not address [the letter] to you, because there is nothing worth writing about.

By including this note in the conclusion of the letter, Pouschine indicated boredom with exile life in Siberia. His confession, "nothing is worth writing about," humbly suggested that his own activities did not deserve Nikoali's attention. His pessimistic outlook evoked discontent with his monotonous life. While Arzamasians celebrated leisurely living, Pouschine was frustrated by such ease, given the absence of noble cause and social purpose.[115] Further, he suggested the circular effects of this issue; having nothing to write about in his own life prevented him from occupying his time with correspondence.

When describing other people's activities, Ivan's tone tended to be more expressive. When describing his decision to send away his daughter Annushka, Ivan made bold, enthusiastic assertions. Ivan evidenced his active interest in Annushka's departure by noting his emotional engagement with the event. He described feeling gratitude «я только должен благодарить» ("I should only thank") for God and faith «с полной уверенностью» ("full of assuredness") while preparing his daughter for the journey. He was «жаль» ("sad") that Nikolai had only a limited opportunity to participate.[116] His invigoration indicated sincere attachment to his family's activities. He appeared to be stimulated by these pursuits, and this stimulation resulted in both emotional sensation as well as physical occupation – preparing his daughter for departure. His recognizable concern also facilitated an intimate connection with his brother.

Ivan also captured Nikolai's interest by defying his brother's expectations as he describes other people's lives. For example, Ivan reported on the illness of M. Bronnikova, the owner of the house in which Pouschine lived with Obolensky in Yalutorovsk. His description aroused Nikolai's intrigue by playing with his expectations of her condition, stating:

«Ты знал её бодрою, деятельною женщиной, а теперь она и без руки и без ноги, и без глаз»![117]

You knew her as a vigorous, active woman, and now she can no longer use her hands, legs, or eyes!

The contrast between her prior and current states imbued the letter with a dramatic tone. Ivan utilized his intimate knowledge of Nikolai's expectations to impart a stimulating reading experience. He assumed Nikolai's past knowledge – thus displaying a strong understanding between the brothers, and refreshed it with shocking present circumstances. The unusual phrasing further reflected the surprising nature of the news. The unconventional description «без руки и без ноги, и без глаз!» dramatized this development through its jarring implications.

He thus established surprise through the content and style of the sentence, and reaffirmed this intent with the exclamation point.

Ivan revealed his reverence for his brother by writing effusively affectionate conclusions. These highly affectionate farewells validated the importance of the recipient to the author. Todd has explained that letters' conclusions are precarious, as they must conclude the letter while also encouraging further conversation.[118] Accordingly, Ivan addressed both objectives by writing expressive gestures intertwined with his lingering curiosities about others:

> «Обнимаю тебе, Марью Николаевну. Целую деток ваших. К Eudoxie пишу казенным путем. Расцелуй всю семью. Может быть, нынешнюю зиму Марья Яковлевна увидится с Аннушкой. Теперь она от вас недалеко будет».[119]

I hug you, Marya Nikolaevna. I kiss your children. To Eudoxie I write by official means. I kiss the whole family. Maybe, this winter Marya Yakovlevna will see you with Annushka. She will not be far from you.

Pouschine often professed his compassion for others. He confirmed his love for his family with physical gestures (kissing and hugging). The repetition of "kiss[ing]" the family emphasized his exuberant attitude, offering an effusive display of love.

Pouschine's familial letters also confirmed his concern for others. He commented on Eudoxie (the son of Decembrist I. D. Yakushkin) and M. Yakovlevna, a family acquaintance. Pouschine established continuity by establishing expectation and arousing excitement for future engagements. Thus, the friendly nature of the conclusion confirmed Ivan's affable outlook, while still humbly directing attention away from himself.

Ultimately, Pouschine's play with epistolary conventions

expressed his modesty endearingly by deemphasizing his own importance. He treated letter writing with great humility as his style highlighted his appreciation for others over his own interests. Throughout his correspondence, Pouschine earnestly sourced intrigue from other people: he briefly noted his own mundane daily activities, while describing other people's news much more expressively. His simple introductions and conclusions showed his gratitude for others; he acknowledged the aid of those delivering the letters as well as his appreciation for his readers, his brother Nikolai, and his family. Pouschine's style in these letters reveals that he placed a high value on friendship. While he used many techniques of the Arzamasians, his letters were distinct in that they acknowledged fulfilling personal connections rather than intellectual life. He thus framed letter writing as a means of attaining consolation, for he used letters to express sincere concern for others.

Family Content

The content of the letters between Ivan and Nikolai – centered on the departure of Pouschine's illegitimate daughter, Annushka, to St. Petersburg – was remarkable for Ivan's display of magnanimity towards his daughter. This moment was significant as Ivan transitioned from an active father to a passive one: rather than raising Annushka himself, he was now sending her to live independently. Throughout his commentary, Ivan's compassionate character was accentuated as he celebrated his family. He forwent discussion of intellectual themes that would more likely interest posterity; rather, he exhibited personal faithfulness to his family, close friends, and God. His attitude towards his role as a father combined the Lyceum's joyous, lighthearted tone with the Decembrists' gravity. Overall, he exhibited affection, sympathy, and devotion.

The role of a father differs considerably from that of a friend, as fathers have an inherent authority and family members cannot be chosen. Yet Pouschine, in his writing, adopted an approach to fatherhood that embodied Decembrist ideals of friendship (i.e. he used relationships to inspire individuals to become better selves and better citizens). Accordingly, he supports Annushka's improvement through advancing her education, and he displays his own willingness to sacrifice the presence of his companion in the name of improving society at large. In recounting the developments to Nikolai, Ivan confirmed the emotional comfort he gained from carrying out this transition; yet the source of this comfort evolved over the course of the correspondence. Though he initially felt satisfaction from action in accordance with his own values, he ultimately described solace stemming from his spiritual sense of righteousness for having made the right decision. Pouschine indicated that his paternal duty was to empower his children to support society's most noble causes, even if that meant sending his daughter away.

Discussing Annushka's departure for St. Petersburg, Ivan displayed his own magnanimous outlook as he praised her devotion to civic causes. First, he affirmed that she would serve society through active work. He praised her new role working in an institute of education. In the following months, he commented on the success of her pursuit:

«Она дельно начала заниматься делом».[120]

She has begun to deal with business efficiently.

Pouschine valued Annushka's ability to achieve pragmatic purpose; in accordance with his earnest attitude, he emphasized the effort associated with her work. The phrase "to deal with business" left her actual work ambiguous, but Ivan emphasized that she acted. Nonetheless, the designation "efficiently" confirmed her success in this role, at least in her father's eyes and in accordance with his values.

Ivan also applauded Annushka's ability to quell emotional stress through her adoring presence. He described her emotional duty to serve a comforting purpose in St. Petersburg: filling the void left from the deaths of a friend's husband and daughter. Ivan notes that the friend will «принимает ее, как дочь[121]» "accept [Annushka] like a daughter" and that one of her companions «лелеяла» ("cherished") Annushka and «не хотел бы разлюбить» ("did not want to fall out love.")[122] Annushka's ability to contribute to society with emotional amelioration reflected the intimate purpose of familial relations. Ivan thus framed Annushka as an instrument through which he could advance his own values. Just as she served a means of transmission for the Lyceum spirit, she also propagated his righteousness, as her new relationships appeared more akin to beneficial familial relations, given her role as "like a daughter." While she primarily acted as a passive vehicle for understanding the Lyceum, she now proved her own agency with her ability to forge loving relationships independently.

Ivan described his role in Annushka's departure, as he attained comfort from confirming her physical and emotional well-being through correspondence. He portrayed the sense of meaning he attained from correspondence, as letters provided him with valuable knowledge of Annushka's development. On the one hand, he corresponded directly with Annushka to validate her own growth:

> «Она здорова, часто имею от нее весточки отрадные. Понимает, как должно, пользу разлуки – и старается настоящим образом воспользоваться случаем

образоваться».[123]

> She's healthy, often I get welcome news from her. She understands, how she should, to favor separation– and to genuinely try to take advantage of this opportunity to develop herself.

Although he has relinquished authority over his daughter, Ivan still appeared to be gratified by confirmations of her beneficial presence.

Ivan's active pursuit of goodwill extended beyond his own family, as he expresses his soulful gratitude for God and the higher, spiritual realm in general. In his letters, Ivan referenced serving his close relatives, but also positioned himself as a devout son of God and devoted brother of man. When facing the decision to send Annushka away to St. Petersburg, he expressed a deep trust in the higher realm. He describes his appreciation of fate for granting them the opportunity to send Annushka to live with M. A. Dorokhova, the widow of a fellow Decembrist:

> «Тут просто действует Провидение, и я только должен благодарить бога и добрую женщину. Теперь подготовляю, что нужно для дороги, и с полной уверенностью провожу Аннушку. Может быть, бог даст, и сам когда-нибудь ее увижу за Уралом».[124]

> It is simply Providence acting, and I only should thank God and the bright woman. Now I prepare what is needed for the road, and with full assurance I guide Annushka. Maybe God will grant me to see her myself sometime before the Urals.

Ivan showed gratitude by directly thanking providence, as well as by deriving consoling "assurance" from carrying out God's will. He acknowledged a sense of submission in fostering family relations: he was willing to set aside his own interests, keeping his daughter at home for companionship, in order to do what he believed was favored by the spiritual realm. Ultimately, his righteous decision proved gratifying as it provided him soulful consolation and demonstrated his magnanimity.

Ivan's chosen content for his letters emphasized selfless intentions given his active praise of Annushka's independence. He celebrated her ability to act for the benefit of society as a whole. However, in contrast to the Arzamasian's use of content to reveal individuality, Ivan instead demonstrated his humble support for soulful well-being. His role was largely passive, as he supported Annushka's ability to contribute to society and relied on correspondence to experience vicarious gratification from her achievements. Ivan praised her dedication to active citizenship, ensured her personal well-being, and praised God in celebration of this opportunity and its resulting soulful consolation. In all, Pouschine demonstrated his gratifying solace in actively encouraging Annushka's righteous work.

Family Conclusion

The family emerges in Pouschine's correspondence as a unique emotional community given its members' shared interest in the general, spiritual well-being of other individuals. Ivan and Nikolai showed appreciation for each other's willingness to perform a wide variety of deeds to protect each other's emotional comfort. Ivan demonstrated appreciation for Annushka through her dedication to continuing his efforts to support society, both practically and emotionally. While the Pouschine family often faced strained relations, Ivan's letters celebrated the loyalty of these two relatives. And while Ivan often faced hardship due to his solitude in Siberia, his deeply intimate relations with family members clearly provided a sense of satisfaction in sharing his deep concern for others. Ultimately, this emotional support enabled Pouschine's righteous decisions – particularly sending Annushka to St. Petersburg – and provided him soulful gratification.

Annushka's departure from Siberia reflected the strong support underlying Ivan's lasting familial relations. The moment both proved his deep love for Annushka, as he sacrificed his companion to enable her to live a better life, and showed his deep intimacy with Nikolai. Ivan appreciated his family for enabling him to feel that he was a good citizen. In the letters, he honed an increasingly poignant relationship with Nikolai: he showed increasing comfort in acknowledging emotional struggles and sharing heavy burdens with his brother. Ivan's style of letters humbly honored other people's pursuits for improving society; accordingly, he underscored his regard for others. He gained consolation through reflecting on their supportive deeds and attitudes, and he appreciated their work. Finally, the unifying theme of Annushka's departure allowed Ivan to share his changing purpose as a father. He became increasingly passive while applauding her improving personal capabilities. Accordingly, Ivan humbly portrayed his role as a family member as a source of support for his relatives, his community, and humanity in general.

The familial emotional community proved unique in its dedication to emotional support. This unifying objective proved more ambiguous than that of the other groups, given the absence of underlying ideology. While the Decembrists sought political improvements, and the Lyceum sought cultural enhancement, the family sought to rectify its members' emotional suffering. Typically, this family's actions involved sharing mutual sympathy and celebrating personal development rather than broadly reshaping Russian society.

In part, this distinction may have resulted from the unique nature of family. First, the family unit comes about as a result of birth, and not as the result of likeminded values. Thus, the family will not necessarily have a specific motivator that catalyzes a connection between two individuals. Second, the generational divide is more significant in the family. For example, Pouschine shifted his role from caretaker to distant supporter of his newly independent daughter. This obligation to relinquish his active role in her life resulted in his attaining gratification from her development rather than from his own actions. Nonetheless, the continued care and consolation Ivan received from his family testified to the deep intimacy of these ties, which enabled him to express profound solace: just as he passively submitted to God's will as a Christian, he also made sacrificial decisions on behalf of the greater well-being of his family. Ultimately, family relations proved gratifying for enabling Pouschine to trust that his values would be actively supported by a force greater than him as an individual.

Conclusion

Ivan Pouschine's correspondence provides an intimate portrayal of his exile by revealing his reliance on friendships for consoling emotional support. Using his correspondence as a reflection of how he related to three distinct emotional communities, we can account for the multifaceted nature of his worldview and the development of his attitudes, especially later in his life. This book, unlike an objective biography, has investigated the complex – and at times, conflicting – aspects of his character. It has analyzed his letters to understand specific examples of how he related to both his proximate surroundings and his most cherished friends. It has also investigated the different outlooks within one man by exploring how he presented himself differently in three different spheres.

By using the structure of emotional communities, Pouschine often did not act solely of his own volition, but rather in response to others. This book has explored the effects of his contact with others: it follows these ongoing relationships and how they led him to attain a sense of purpose in his own life.

Ultimately, Pouschine's pursuit of a common desired emotion with a friend inspired him to involve himself in the Siberian community. He occupied his time by assisting in governance, playing music, and arranging educational opportunities for his children. While this book has explored only a portion of Pouschine's diverse efforts, it has nonetheless related the general purposes of friendship, especially at the emotionally strenuous end of his exile.

Reflecting his youthful, patriotic spirit, Pouschine sought to occupy himself with the progressive reform of Russia's sociopolitical situation. He related to the fellow Decembrist Yakushkin by reflecting on moments that offered a sense of triumph for the group's efforts in Siberia, despite the catastrophic failure of their rebellion. His writing style in letters to Yakushkin was stoic and solemn, underscoring the stately intentions of Decembrist actions. However, he nonetheless showed his emotional concern for his Decembrist friends by using affectionate language and including amiable messages. Ultimately, his friendship with Yakushkin provided Pouschine with an internal sense of power. His Decembrist friendships served to gratify Pouschine's desire to have a significant and positive effect on the management of Siberian society.

Pouschine's Lyceum friendships aided him sentimentally by elating his general spirit while he was Siberia. By the end of his exile, Pouschine suffered notably from acute solitude. He relied on his bright Lyceum memories to provide a motivating sense of delight in his life. In addition to attaining joy from the memories themselves, he honored nostalgic tokens that validated his memories: portraits, the gifted piano, and the Lyceum song. The Lyceum group bonded over their exuberant joy for resurrecting elements of their blissful school days. He presented his bliss by incorporating lyrics into letters, underscoring their poignancy. The piano – gifted to Pouschine as a result of the letters – enabled him to revive the Lyceum song, and to bestow this joy upon his daughter.

Finally, Pouschine's correspondence with his family prompted him to display active concern for the spiritual stability of others. While the Lyceum group added joy to society, the family group mitigated emotional struggle. Pouschine and his brother Nikolai often discussed the emotional state of dear friends in attempts to quell soulful distress. They bonded over their shared dedication to carrying out action that was worthy of appreciation. Indeed, the brothers responded with thankfulness and pointing out further opportunities for aid. Their writing style was marked by affectionate greetings and messages that underscored the brothers' concern for each other. Furthermore, the religious references throughout their correspondence underscored the spiritual nature of their ambitions. In the most Christian sense of brotherhood, Nikolai and Ivan celebrated the divine consolation arising from righteous action. Pouschine's decision to separate from his daughter was evidence of his willingness to sacrifice his comforting companionship to advance her personal and professional development, and ultimately society as a whole. Pouschine thus proved his commitment to making decisions righteously. Nonetheless, his reliance on Nikolai for consolation demonstrated the soulfully supportive role of his family relationships.

Pouschine relied on letters to inspire himself and his friends to address noble causes in society. On one hand, this approach reflected the past role of epistolary correspondence in Russian society. As described by Todd, the Arzamasians used their correspondence to discuss and develop their attitudes towards enlightened ideas. The progressive intentions of their ongoing correspondence proved to be a commonality between them and Pouschine, and thus between these two periods.

On the other hand, however, Pouschine diverged from the Arzamasians given the desire for emotional consolation – rather than intellectual intrigue – underlying the letters. Pouschine relied on correspondence as a primary means of socialization, whereas for many of the Arzamasians, letters were supplementary to actual engagement. Pouschine used letters to advance his friendships rather than bolstering his social image or intellectual reputation. The letters showed that Pouschine placed a greater emphasis on his own consolation and improving his own surroundings than he did on providing something interesting for posterity.

While Pouschine discussed a variety of occupations and ambitions, he never veered from the pursuit of righteousness. Across all efforts, he displayed his relentless drive to support others' well-being. He found solace in moments when his connections with others contributed to Russia's advancement. This outlook reflected Pouschine's continued adherence to the patriotic spirit that was initially aroused in his early Lyceum education. He appears to have found a sense of purpose in inspiring others to become better and more active citizens, and thus better men. Pouschine's letters show how one can transcend the consequences of an unfortunate life choice – and the despondency of solitude – by engaging members of communities that shared an emotional pursuit. Consolation resulted from friendships when it enabled someone to be sure that their actions were indeed able to benefit society as a whole. And, as proven by the impeccable care with which Pouschine preserved these letters, correspondence was a meaningful pursuit for him in his loneliness. He was gratified by the confirmation that he could still be a productive member of his society. Although his efforts by necessity had to become subtle and even obscure after the Decembrist Uprising, he nonetheless demonstrated great personal diligence by continuing to promote righteousness and responsibility for the future of Russia.

Afterward

The ascent of Tsar Alexander II to the throne in 1855 brought the exiled Decembrists amnesty. Part of the new ruler's anticipated program of reform, which would soon implement the abolition of serfdom among numerous other measures, after his coronation in August 1856, the Decembrists were pardoned and released from their sentences of "eternal servitude;" allowed to return to European Russia; and had their rights, privileges, and titles restored. The surviving able-bodied Decembrists left Siberia and reestablished themselves in cities they had not seen since the uprising.

Ivan Pouschine returned to St. Petersburg in December 1856. His life after exile was marked by a resurgence of companionship: in May 1857, he married Natalya Dimitrievna Fonvizina, widow of the Decembrist Mikhail Aleksandrovich Fonvizin. Pouschine and Fonvizina's relationship had formed in the early 1840s, when Pouschine stayed with the Fonvizins several times in their settlement in Tobol'sk. The strength of the closeness and mutual trust between Pouschine and Fonvizina was immediate and clear; she later became one of the few people who knew the identity of the mother of Pouschine's illegitimate son Vania. The nature of their relationship changed dramatically after the death of Mikhail Aleksandrovich Fonvizin in 1853; it became intimate as they began a two-year "romance in letters." Their correspondence was marked by beautifully crafted professions of love that displayed Pouschine's resolute devotion to his beloved and singular ability to care for her throughout her periods of passionate fluctuations. The two had a happy marriage.

After marrying Fonvizina, Pouschine lived quietly on her estate in Bronnitsy, outside of Moscow. The marriage brightened his last years with the soulful cheer of intimate connection and material independence. The latter enabled Pouschine to devote himself to write "Notes on Pushkin" («Записки о Пушкине»), a key source of facts, episodes, and stories about the famous poet. Pouschine's memoir portrayed his dear friend with a rare understanding of his personality and remains an important account of Pushkin's young life. And, all the while, Pouschine corresponded with his fellow Decembrists to remember Pushkin, as well as to converse about their returns to European Russia and perspectives on the ongoing changes in Russia more broadly.

Pouschine died on April 3, 1859. He was buried outside the Cathedral of the Archangel Michael in Bronnitsy, near the grave of his wife's first husband Mikhail Fonvizin. Pouschine's two major works—his epistolary collection and *Notes on Pushkin*—continue to provide key insights on the circumstances of daily life for a wide variety of nineteenth-century Russians and immortalize the meaningful bonds of friendship that served to inspire a motivating sense of righteousness.

The Decembrists' enlightened spirit lived on through the reign of Alexander II. The Tsar saw through key progressive reforms that aligned with the Decembrists' aspirations for Russia. Most prominently, he carried out the abolition of serfdom with the Emancipation Act of 1861. His further overhauls included a Westernized judicial system, a system of elected local government, a comprehensive reorganization of the Russian military, and the modernization of Russia's transportation infrastructure.

At the time of Alexander II's assassination in 1881, he was about to sign a manifesto to establish a form of national representative government. The underlying intention of these reforms to advance Russia would have gratified Pouschine and his fellow Decembrists: they enabled new opportunities for Russians to serve their country righteously as beneficial citizens.

Works Cited

"И. Д. Якушкин" Смоленщина XIX век, accessed March 26, 2018, http://shikanov.skbeloh.edusite.ru/jakuchin.htm.

Кремер, Б. А, «Матюшкин Ф. Ф.: биографическая справка», accessed March 26, 2018, http://az.lib.ru/m/matjushkin_f_f/text_0010.shtml.

«Николай Иванович Пущин р. 7 март 1803 ум. 1874» Accessed March 26, 2018. http://az.lib.ru/p/pushin_i_i/text_0010.shtml.

Пущин И. И. *Сочинения и Письма. В 2 т. Т. 1 Записки о Пушкине. Письма 1816-1849 гг.* – М.: Наука, 1999. 551 с.

Пущин И. И. *Сочинения и Письма. В 2 т. Т. 2 Письма 1850-1859 гг.* – М.: Наука, 2001. 624 с.

Русский биографически словарь. В 25 м. Т 15. Притвицъ – Рейсъ. – С. Петербургъ, 1910. 558 с.

Balakin, Alexei. Interview by Anna Pouschine. Princeton, NJ. April 20, 2018.

Peschio, Joeseph. *The Poetics of Impudence and Intimacy in the Age of Pushkin*, Madison: Wisconsin University Press, 2013.

Riasanovsky, Nicholas. "Nicholas I: Tsar of Russia." Encyclopedia Britannica.

Last modified February 23, 2018. Accessed April 7, 2018. https://www.britannica.com/biography/Nicholas-I-tsar-of-Russia.

Rosenwein, Barbara H. *Emotional Communities in the Early Middle Ages*, Ithaca: Cornell University Press, 2006.

Todd, William Mills, III. *The Familiar Letter as a Literary Genre in the Age of Pushkin*. Princeton, NJ: Princeton University Press, 1976.

Wachtell, Michael. *A Commentary to Pushkin's Lyric Poetry, 1826-1836*.

Madison, WI: University of Wisconsin Press, 2011.

Wang, Emily Ambrose. "Civic Feeling: Pushkin and the Decembrist Emotional Community." Ph.D. diss., Princeton University, 2016.

Notes

1 М. П. Мироненко, С. В. Мироненко, «Жизнь и судьба Ивана Пущина», в *И*.

2 Emily Ambrose Wang, "Civic Feeling: Pushkin and the Decembrist Emotional Community" (PhD diss., Princeton University, 2016), 14.

3 Barbara H. Rosenwein, Emotional Communities in the Early Middle Ages, Ithaca: Cornell University Press, 2006, quoted in Emily Ambrose Wang, "Civic Feeling: Pushkin and the Decembrist Emotional Community" (PhD diss., Princeton University, 2016), 16.

4 Wang, "Civic Feeling," 3.

5 Ibid, 3.

6 "И. Д. Якушкин" Смоленщина XIX век, accessed March 26, 2018, http://shikanov.skbeloh.edusite.ru/jakuchin.htm.

7 Wang, "Civic Feeling," 14.

8 Ibid, 39.

9 Ibid, 36.

10 Ibid, 36.

11 Ibid, 34.

12 William Mills Todd, III, *The Familiar Letter as a Literary Genre in the Age of Pushkin* (Princeton, NJ: Princeton University Press, 1976), 72.

13 Ibid, 13.

14 Ibid, 40.

15 Ibid, 54.

16 Ibid, 73.

17 «Эпистолярное Наследие Ивана Пущина», в *И. И. Пущин. Сочинения и письма. В 2 т. Т. 2. Письма 1850-1859 гг.* - Москва: Наука, 2001, с. 10.

18 Мироненко, Мироненко, «Жизнь и судьба», в *И. И. Пущин. Сочинения и письма. В 2 т. Т. 1. Записки о Пушкине. Письма 1816-1849 гг.* - Москва: Наука, 1999, с. 10.

19 Wang, "Civic Feeling," 14-15.

20 Ibid, 14-15.

21 Ibid, 3.

22 Ibid, 26.

23 Ibid, 31.

24 Н. В. Самовер, «И. И. Пущин», в *Русский биографически словарь. В 25 м. Т 15. Притвицъ – Рейсъ.* – С. Петербургъ, 1910, с. 223.

25 Мироненко, Мироненко, «Жизнь и судьба», в *И. И. Пущин*, с. 11.

26 Н. В. Самовер, «И. И. Пущин», в *Русский биографически словарь*, с. 223.

27 Мироненко, Мироненко, «Жизнь и судьба», в *И. И. Пущин*, с. 11.

28 Там же, с. 12.

29 Там же, с. 12.

30 Там же, с. 12.

31 Там же, с. 13.

32 Там же, с. 13.

33 Самовер, «И. И. Пущин», в *Русский биографически словарь*, с. 223.

34 Мироненко, Мироненко, «Жизнь и судьба», в *И. И. Пущин*, с. 23.

35 Самовер, «И. И. Пущин», в *Русский биографически словарь* с. 223.

36 Мироненко, Мироненко, «Жизнь и судьба», в *И. И. Пущин*, с. 25.

37 Там же, с. 25-26.

38 Там же, с. 27.

39 Там же, с. 28.

40 Там же, с. 29.

41 Самовер, «И. И. Пущин», в *Русский биографически словарь* с. 223.

42 Там же, с. 223.

43 Там же с. 223.

44 Мироненко, Мироненко, «Жизнь и судьба», в *И. И. Пущин*, с. 32.

45 "И. Д. Якушкин," Смоленска XIX Века.

46 Там же xlvii Там же

47 Там же

48 Wang, "Civic Feeling," 3.

49 Пущин, И. И. «350. Е. И. и И. Д. Якушкиным» 1885, в *И. И. Пущин*, с. 134- 135.

50 Пущин, И. И. «410. И. Д. Якушкину» 1856, в «*И. И. Пущин*», с. 213-214.

51 Пущин, И. И. «335. И. Д. Якушкину» 1855, в *И. И. Пущин*, 117-119.

52 Там же, с. 117-119

53 Пущин, «350. Е. И. и И. Д. Якушкиным», в *И. И. Пущин*, с. 135.

54 Nicholas Riasanovsky, "Nicholas I: Tsar of Russia," Encyclopedia Brittanica, last modified February 23, 2018, accessed April 7, 2018, https://www.britannica.com/biography/Nicholas-I-tsar-of-Russia.

55 Пущин, «335. И. Д. Якушкину», *И. И. Пущин*, 117-119

56 Там же, с. 117-119

57 Там же, с. 117-119

58 Пущин, «410. И. Д. Якушкину», *И. И. Пущин*, 213-214.

59 Пущин, «335. И. Д. Якушкину», в *И. И. Пущин*, с. 117-119

60 Там же, с. 117-119

61 Пущин, «350. Е. И. и И. Д. Якушкиным», в *И. И. Пущин*, с. 134-135.

62 Пущин, «335. И. Д. Якушкину», в *И. И. Пущин*, с. 117-119

63 Мироненко, Мироненко, «Жизнь и судьба», в *И. И. Пущин*, с. 9.

64 Там же, с. 9.

65 Там же, с. 10.

66 Там же. с. 10.

67 Там же, с. 5-6.

68 Самовер, «И. И. Пущин», в *Русский биографически словарь* с. 223.

69 Wang, "Civic Feeling," 36.

70 Ibid, 34.

71 Мироненко, Мироненко, «Жизнь и судьба», в *И. И. Пущин*, с. 6.

72 Там же с. 6.

73 А. Е. Ельницкий. «И. И. Пущину: биографическая справка», accessed March 26, 2018, http://az.lib.ru/p/pushin_i_i/text_0010.shtml.

74 Peschio, Joeseph, *The Poetics of Impudence and Intimacy in the Age of Pushkin*, Madison: Wisconsin University Press, 2013.

75 Мироненко, Мироненко, «Жизнь и судьба», в *И. И. Пущин*. с. 35.

76 «Эпистолярное Наследие Ивана Пущина», в *И. И. Пущин*, с. 10.

77 Кремер, Б. А, «Матюшкин Ф. Ф.: биографическая справка», accessed March 26, 2018, http://az.lib.ru/m/matjushkin_f_f/text_0010.shtml.

78 Крупская, «Родился Поэт», Президентская Библиотека.

79 Пущин, И. И. «278. Ф. Ф. Матюшкину», в *И. И. Пущин,* с. 59-60.

80 Пущин, И. И. «274. Ф. Ф. Матюшкину», в *И. И. Пущин,* с. 57-58.

81 Там же, с. 57-58.

82 Пущин, «277. Ф. Ф. Матюшкину», в *И. И. Пущин,* с. 57-58.

83 Там же, с. 57-58.

84 Там же, с. 57-58.

85 Там же, с. 57-58.

86 Там же, с. 57-58.

87 Пущин, «278. Ф. Ф. Матюшкину», в *И. И. Пущин,* с. 59-60.

88 Алексей Балакин, interview by Anna Pouschine, Princeton, NJ, April 20, 2018.

89 Ibid

90 Ibid

91 Пущин, «278. Ф. Ф. Матюшкину», в *И. И. Пущин,* с. 59-60.

92 Michael Wachtell, *A Commentary to Pushkin's Lyric Poetry, 1826-1836* (Madison, WI: University of Wisconsin Press, 2011), 41.

93 Ibid, 41.

94 Пущин, «277. Ф. Ф. Матюшкину», в *И. И. Пущин,* с. 57-58.

95 Пущин, «278. Ф. Ф. Матюшкину», в *И. И. Пущин,* с. 59-60.

96 Там же, с. 59-60.

97 Мироненко, Мироненко, «Жизнь и судьба», в *И. И. Пущин,* с. 34.

98 Там же, с. 7.

99 Там же, с. 7.

100 Там же, с. 8.

101 «Эпистолярное Наследие Ивана Пущина», в *И. И. Пущин,* с. 7.

102 Мироненко, Мироненко, «Жизнь и судьба», в *И. И. Пущин,* с. 8.

103 Там же, с. 32-33.

104 Там же, с. 32-33.

105 «Николай Иванович Пущин р. 7 март 1803 ум. 1874» Accessed March 26, 2018. http://az.lib.ru/p/pushin_i_i/text_0010.shtml.

106 Мироненко, Мироненко, «Жизнь и судьба», в *И. И. Пущин*, с. 33.

107 Wang, "Civic Feeling," 30.

108 Пущин, И. И. «385. Н. И. Пущину» 1856, в *И. И. Пущин*, с. 189-190.

109 Пущин, И. И. «357. М. Н. иН. И. Пущиным», в *И. И. Пущин*, с. 141-142.

110 Пущин, И. И. «385. Н. И. Пущину», в *И. И. Пущин* с. 189-190.

111 Пущин, И. И. «351. Н. И. Пущину», в *И. И. Пущин* с. 136-137.

112 Todd, The Familiar, 183.

113 Пущин, И. И. «370. Н. И. Пущину» 1856, в *И. И. Пущин*, с. 160-166.

114 Todd, The Familiar, 98.

115 Пущин, И. И. «346. Н. И. Пущину» 1855, в *И. И. Пущин*, с. 130-132.

116 Пущин, И. И. «357. М. Н. иН. И. Пущиным», в *И. И. Пущин*, с. 141-142.

117 Todd, The Familiar, 176-177.

118 Пущин, И. И. «351. Н. И. Пущину», в *И. И. Пущин*, с. 136-137.

119 Пущин, И. И. «358. Н. И. Пущину», в *И. И. Пущин*, с. 142-143.

120 Пущин, И. И. «346. Н. И. Пущину», в *И. И. Пущин*, с. 130-132.

121 Пущин, И. И. «370. Н. И. Пущину», в *И. И. Пущин*, с. 165-166.

122 Пущин, И. И. «357. М. Н. и Н. И. Пущиным», в *И. И. Пущин*, с. 141-142.

123 Пущин, И. И. «346. Н. И. Пущину» 1855, в *И. И. Пущин*, с. 130-132.

www.ingramcontent.com/pod-product-compliance
Lightning Source LLC
Chambersburg PA
CBHW071851230426
43671CB00012B/2141